Appendices **162**

A Notes for partners **163**
B Notes for professionals **171**

Resources **176**

Sources of help **177**
Further reading and films
featuring CSA **182**
Useful organisations **185**

The Warrior Within

A One in Four handbook to aid recovery from childhood sexual abuse and violence

Christiane Sanderson

Our thanks

One in Four

We publish this book in recognition of those survivors who have already found a voice and in the hope that it will assist those still on their journey to achieve a successful outcome.

Our thanks to all of you who have made this possible.

This book would not have been possible without the support and commitment of those identified by the author and thanked by her in her personal acknowledgements.

Finally, and most importantly, our thanks and appreciation go to our author Christiane Sanderson who has given to us generously both of her time and expertise which in the future will be of lasting benefit – to both each survivor as an individual and to the charity as a whole.

Andrew Andrews MBE
Chairman of Trustees

Second edition
Text © Christiane Sanderson and One in Four
Title, design, layout and format © One in Four

Published by One in Four, 219 Bromley Rd, Catford SE6 2PG · Telephone 020 8697 2112 · Email admin@oneinfour.org.uk
Printed and bound by Circle Services Group
All rights reserved. No part of this publication may be reproduced, stored in a retrieval system, or transmitted in any form or by any means, electronic, mechanical, photocopying, recording or otherwise, without prior permission from the copyright holders
ISBN 978-0-9566541-2-0

Author's acknowledgements

Dedication

To all survivors of childhood sexual abuse and sexual violence, and my mother Gertrude Auer who taught me about courage and the warrior within.

Acknowledgements

I would like to thank Linda Dominguez, the Director of One in Four, for her commitment and enthusiasm and for inviting me to write this handbook. This project would not have come to fruition without the help of Andrew Andrews MBE, Dianne Ludlow, Verna Harris, Conny Looi Osborne, Laura Joanknecht, Marie Davies and all the staff and counsellors at One in Four. A huge thank you too, to Awards for All for funding this project. Thanks also go to Nine Rogers and Steve Bucke for design and production of the handbook, to Wendy Allchin for dedication in proofreading and to Paul Glyn, Mary Davies and Elwyn Taylor for their helpful feedback. Finally, I could not have written this book without the unwavering support of Michael, James and Max.

How to get the most from this handbook

Congratulations! To have got this far and be reading this book means you have survived your childhood sexual abuse (CSA). The warrior within has served you well. Take a moment to acknowledge and validate how far you have come and plan how you can celebrate this. You could light a candle, share your journey so far with a trusted friend, go out for or prepare a special meal, go to a concert, have a party or perform a ceremony or ritual that is meaningful to you. You could consider purchasing something that symbolises your survival so far. This could be a small piece of jewellery such as a ring, brooch or pendant that can be worn every day, or a small object that is easily carried, or an inspirational image or quote on your mobile phone. Whatever you choose let it be a reminder of your survival and a symbol of your strength and courage; your warrior within.

Your warrior within

Your warrior has fought for your survival and succeeded in bringing you to this point of healing. The definition of warrior is *'a person engaged or experienced in warfare... who shows or has shown great vigour or courage.'* Child sexual abuse is like living in a war zone and it takes tremendous courage and resilience to survive such brutalising warfare. Your warrior has defended and protected you and will continue to be an important resource in your recovery.

Your journey

Surviving the dehumanising effects of CSA takes tremendous strength and courage. Reading this handbook shows that, despite being betrayed, hope has not been destroyed. Your warrior is still alive and believes that things can change and that you can recover. The aim of the handbook is to honour the warrior within and to put you back in control of your life and your healing. It will provide you with additional support to take ownership of your recovery. As a result, you will be able to loosen the power others have or had over you and make you less dependent on them. This will help you to gain greater control over the effects of CSA and improve the quality of your life.

Ultimately, your recovery will allow you to relegate the CSA to the past so that it no longer dictates who you are and how to live your life. As you do this, you will move from surviving to thriving and begin to live a more fulfilling and personally meaningful life.

Your resources

To have survived so far means that you already have a number of valuable resources, not least your warrior within. Take a moment to think about the strengths your warrior has which have helped you to survive so far. This handbook will help you to identify these more clearly and build upon them. As you can begin to take greater control over your recovery, you will rediscover aspects of yourself that have gone into hiding, and reclaim these to become who you were meant to be. Your warrior within will become your inspiration so that you can restore the qualities that you most admire yet have had to deny. It is these qualities that will help you to focus your resources and put you back in control to choose what is right for you rather than have that dictated by others, To support this the handbook merely offers guidance NOT compulsory instruction.

Restoring reality

Restoring reality is the path to recovery, and it is important to acknowledge and legitimise your CSA experiences. The handbook will help you to make sense of your CSA from your own perspective and reality and challenge what you have been told to think and feel. It will replace the abuser's reality with your own reality. This will help you to trust yourself and your reality. Once you are able to trust yourself more you will regain trust in others and reconnect to the world. To do this you need to feel safe to choose what is right for you and how you want to live.

Taking control

In taking control of your recovery you will be able to invest in your growth and commit to trusting yourself. While this will be exhausting and overwhelming at times, the handbook will act as a companion or portable therapist to keep you on track. It will act as a reminder that the effects of CSA can be reversed by reclaiming the very human qualities that the abuse has tried to destroy. Trust, empathy, compassion, love, caring and nurturing will resurface, along with kindness in giving and receiving, so that joy and pleasure in being alive will be experienced. By reclaiming these you will be able to embrace rather than retreat from yourself, others and life, to restore the connections that are vital to your sense of well-being. In this, you and your warrior will finally triumph over trauma.

Structure of the handbook

The book is divided into three parts with **part one** focusing on understanding childhood sexual abuse and its impact by looking at the importance of safety, understanding the nature of childhood sexual abuse and trauma and your reactions to it, as well as the process of healing and obstacles to recovery.

Part two identifies how to manage your reactions to trauma, by examining how to restore control, how to manage sensations and feelings, flashbacks, panic attacks, nightmares, dissociation, negative thoughts and memories. It will also look at harmful behaviours such as self- injury, alcohol and substance misuse, as well as how to manage relationships and sexual difficulties, and the role of loss and grieving in recovering from CSA.

Part three builds upon what has been learnt so far and emphasises how to rebuild your life by restoring your reality, maintaining self-care, preventing relapse and restoring relationships. It will also look at how to go about seeking justice, how to reconnect to life and the importance of post-traumatic growth. The **appendices** include guidance for partners, friends or family of survivors and professionals who may wish to read this handbook. In addition, there is a list of **resources** such as helpful organisations, further reading and helpful films.

How to use the handbook

The handbook is for both female and male survivors of CSA and sexual violence, whether abused by a male or female abuser, either within or outside the family, or in a religious context. It is designed in such a way that you can dip in and out of it as you need to. You do not have to read all the sections or read them in order. It is a flexible resource to be used in the way it most suits you. It is not designed to replace counselling, or the enormous value of a therapeutic relationship. It can, however, enable you to create a safe, secure base within you that allows you to become more sensitively attuned to yourself and your needs. I hope you will find it useful as well as inspirational and that it can bring comfort when most needed.

Key to icons

 REMEMBER

 WARNING

 TOP TIP

 EXERCISE

 ACTIVITY

⚠️ **WARNING** It is essential to create safety before reading the handbook. You must make sure that you go at your own pace and know how to brake and accelerate. If reading the handbook, or doing any one of the exercises, becomes too uncomfortable STOP reading the book or doing the activity. Do something soothing or grounding that is enjoyable and that brings you pleasure. Only return to reading or the activity when you feel ready.

Getting started

✏️ **EXERCISE** To help you get started, buy an '**activity journal**' – a notebook or folder in which to record your feelings and thoughts as you work through the handbook. It is also a useful place to record and monitor your recovery, including what works, what makes you feel better and any setbacks. This journal of your recovery can be either a diary, a lined exercise book, a blank notebook, a scrapbook, a selection of coloured paper, which can be put into a folder, a document on your computer, a photo album or something that you make yourself. You might wish to customise the cover with images, words or symbols that represent you, or your warrior, and your healing journey. If you are self-conscious or anxious about writing you can draw, or record your entries onto a CD, MP3 player, mobile phone or video.

💡 **TOP TIP** After each entry reflect on what you have recorded and list three things that you have in your life that you are grateful for and express your gratitude.

Remember to record things in your journal that are inspirational and that give you pleasure and hope, as well as your difficult times. These can be copies of favourite paintings, drawings or images, poems or quotes. It is important to include good memories, feelings and thoughts to counterbalance the more negative ones. If you prefer to draw then make sure you have lots of coloured paper, pens and paint and a folder to store them in.

⚠️ **WARNING** If you are not in a safe environment where your journal, recordings or artwork can be found then see if you can find a safe place to store them such as a trusted friend or professional.

✏️ **EXERCISE** A good way to start your journal is by making a list of contact details of all those in your **support network**. This should include professionals such as your GP, counsellor, support worker, social

9

worker, useful organisations such as One in Four or Samaritans, as well as trusted friends and family. List phone numbers, and email addresses along with best times to make contact. It might be useful to include numbers that can help in an emergency when you are not able to contact those in your support network, such as One in Four 020 8697 2112 or Samaritans 08457 90 90 90. It is also helpful to note the particular skills that friends and family possess and how they can best support you, either practically or emotionally so you can contact the one that is best for you at any point in your recovery.

EXERCISE Your next entry could be an image or **metaphor** of your healing. This can consist of an inspirational image, such as your warrior within, or a collage of favourite images that symbolise well being and healing to you. Finding a metaphor is particularly useful especially if it is something that resonates with you. Some common examples include the warrior within, gardening, building a house or car, writing a book or play with you as the author, making music, directing a film with you as director, managing a sports team, or clearing an overflowing cupboard or drawer (see **Understanding the process of recovery and healing** on page 39).

To help you identify what recovery means to you, you could also list some of the things that you associate with well being and living in a more meaningful way. If it is hard to put this into words, then make a collage of images, or a compilation of music that you find soothing or uplifting.

 EXERCISE Make a list of your strengths and resources that have helped you to survive. These are really important to acknowledge and build upon. Next make a list of specific goals that will enable you to make changes within yourself, your relationships, your work and your home life. To help you, divide these goals into manageable units of time. For example *'My goals in the next three months... six months... one year... two years... and five years...'* Try to be realistic in what you hope to achieve, and make a note of any potential obstacles. Be mindful of what can and cannot be changed and focus your energy on what can change. Tick off each goal when you have achieved it. Remind yourself that the process of recovery will include obstacles and setbacks and when these occur be compassionate to yourself, revise your timeline and specific goals.

REMEMBER This is a work in progress and your goals can change, and you can add and subtract as you gain more knowledge and progress.

It is just as important to be committed to your healing as it is to achieve recovery. Do not rush your recovery but pace it to suit what you can manage and build upon each step. It is better to take one step and one day at a time rather than rushing the ultimate goal. To this effect it is more beneficial to do a little, but often. Make a commitment to yourself to write regularly in your journal, and practise those exercises that are most helpful to you. Remember change is not easy, nor is acquiring new skills. It is only through practise that new skills are integrated into your life allowing old, destructive habits to fade. You can savour each small step in your recovery by reflecting regularly on what works for you and your progress.

EXERCISE Make a list of pleasurable and positive activities that make you feel better and transform your mood such as smiling, singing, listening to music, keeping in touch with trusted friends, even if only by text or email, walking, swimming, or going to a concert or gallery. Decide to do at least one on your list each day, and some of the others at least once a week.

REMEMBER No one exercise or activity works for all. You can decide what is useful for you and what does not work without feeling bad. It is better to focus on what works rather than forcing yourself to adopt all of them.

Safety contract

If you are feeling suicidal, or have attempted suicide and feel you may do so again, you need to make a safety contract with a trusted friend or a professional. You need to make an agreement, preferably written and signed by you and the other person, that if you feel that you are a danger to yourself that you will contact them and discuss how you are feeling before proceeding. You will also need to seek additional professional support such as counselling. Keep the contact details of the trusted friend or professional along with the number for Samaritans easily to hand, or store in your mobile phone under 'emergency'.

WARNING If you are feeling suicidal contact a trusted friend, your GP, counsellor or Samaritans 08457 90 90 90.

Part one
Understanding childhood sexual abuse as trauma

1 Safety first

Before starting on your journey of recovery it is important to create as much safety as possible in your life. This will protect you when you experience overwhelming trauma reactions and help you to feel more in control over your trauma related reactions, physical sensation and emotions. Safety will also help you to regulate your moods states so that you can improve your well-being and quality of life.

How safe are you?

To assess how safe you are you will need to check to what extent you feel safe in your environment (**external safety**) and how much you are able to control trauma related reactions (**internal safety**). External safety is dependent on being in a safe place with access to the basic necessities critical to your daily life. These include a safe place to live, adequate food and clothing and good quality support from trusted others. Internal safety is when you experience a degree of control over your feelings, sensations and thoughts.

WARNING If you have uncontrollable and frequent thoughts of suicide or are actively suicidal then stop reading the handbook and seek professional help.

You will not feel safe if you are still living with or are dependent on your abuser or abusers, are in an abusive relationship, or totally isolated from others. If you are in an unsafe environment it will be important to seek additional support or help (see **Resources** on page 176). Your internal safety is dependent on how well you are able to function and manage in your everyday life. If you are able to get up, perform daily tasks, have some control over your anxieties and intrusive memories and are able to regulate your mood, then you have a degree of internal safety. If however you feel out of control, at the mercy of intrusive thoughts, flashbacks, nightmares or panic attacks, or frequently dissociate, then you are not safe. You are also not safe if you engage in self-destructive behaviours such as self-injury or substance misuse to regulate your mood. While this handbook aims to help you learn the skills to establish internal safety, you might consider seeking additional sources of support such as a counsellor or a survivor group.

REMEMBER This handbook does not replace the value of counselling or therapy but is an additional source of help and support. You can use it alongside your work with your counsellor or support group, or use it as a stepping stone to seek counselling or support.

If you feel safe enough to continue reading this handbook you will discover ways to manage both external and internal safety which will enable you to develop additional skills to gain more control over your trauma reactions and regulate your feelings. To make this easier it is important to identify those things that calm and soothe you that will prove to be invaluable on your journey to recovery.

ACTIVITY Many survivors find creating a **mood basket** or **mood box** a helpful way to regulate their feelings and mood. A mood basket is particularly useful as it can be easily transported between rooms or locations, while a box with a lock will ensure greater privacy. Find a nice basket or box, which you can customise, and place things into it that calm you, bring you pleasure or which you find inspirational. These can include calming images, cards or postcards, meaningful pebbles, stones, or crystals, favourite photographs, flowers or your favourite music CDs. Other items could include a favourite DVD, book, poem or quotation, a calming scent or aroma, objects from a time or place associated with good memories, jewellery from a loved one, a piece of cloth or a soft toy.

What you put in your mood basket will be unique and meaningful to you. The only guideline is that it helps you to change your mood when you are feeling sad, overwhelmed or anxious. Start by creating the basket with items already in your possession and gradually add any other meaningful items that will help you on your journey. Ideally it helps to include items that stimulate all of the five senses: smell, sight, sound, touch and taste.

Music

Music is a powerful way to regulate emotions and feelings. You could consider making a number of music compilations to help you regulate your mood including uplifting and energising music, as well as calming and relaxing music. These can be stored as playlists on an MP3 player or mobile phone so that they are easily accessible. The playlists can reflect a range of moods from calming, to energising and invigorating, to music that will channel your anger. You could also make a memory based playlist to help you when recalling blocked memories.

WARNING Do not play memory based music until you have mastered a range of mood regulation and grounding skills.

Anchors

In creating your mood basket you will have identified some objects that can help to anchor you in moments of distress. Anchors are any objects that ground you and represent a feeling of safety such as a pebble, stone, coin or crystal. It is especially helpful if your anchor is associated with the present day and did not exist in the past when the trauma occurred. A good example of this is an MP3 player or mobile phone which you would not have had when you were a child. These can be particularly helpful during flashbacks and dissociation to orient yourself in the present, and to record instructions to help you to manage disorienting episodes (see **Managing flashbacks, nightmares, panic attacks and dissociation** on page 70).

It helps if the anchor is portable so that you can carry it around with you at all times. Another powerful anchor is a comforting smell such as favourite scent, aftershave or aroma. Make sure that the smell reminds you of when you have felt safe and is associated with comfort and well-being. You can release your comforting smell by lighting a scented candle, leaving spices in a bowl in your room, or spraying the scent or aftershave onto a scarf or piece of clothing.

Oasis and safe place

Two other powerful sources to help you regulate your mood is having an **oasis** and **safe place** to which you can go to when you feel overwhelmed. These will be activities or places that will ground and soothe you.

EXERCISE In your journal make a list of activities, people or places that are associated with pleasure and which have a calming and soothing effect on you. You might also include some that you find uplifting and invigorating and which restore a sense of well-being. These will form the basis of your oases and safe place. You can collect images of these and put them into your mood basket to use as required. Your oases could include activities that help you to relax such as having a warm bath, massage, meditation, sitting in the sunshine in the park, reading, watching a film, listening to music, going to a concert, or watching or playing sport. Alongside this you could identify a grounding position which is comforting such as curling up, squatting or lying down with a favourite blanket. You may find it uncomfortable to relax and so prefer invigorating activities that are a source of pleasure such as swimming, exercising, playing sports, dancing, singing, going for a walk or running.

Once you have listed these, identify those that you could easily integrate into your life and make a commitment to engage in these activities regularly so that they become an established part of your daily life.

Next think of a safe place, past or present, which has been, is or could be, a site of protection. If there has never been a safe place in your life, then try to imagine one. Whether real or imagined, it is helpful to associate as many sensory cues as you can to this safe place – the smells, the sounds, the feel, the sights and the taste. In writing down as many things associated with this safe place you will be able to enter it whenever you need to.

Once you have identified your anchor, oases and safe place, you will be able to use these while reading this book and throughout your recovery. From now on you will be able to regulate your distress and uncomfortable feelings by using your anchor, oases or safe place to soothe and comfort you. Knowing how to counterbalance negative feelings with more positive ones will enable you to improve the quality of your everyday life. These basic skills will help you to take more control of your trauma related reactions which lead to a greater sense of safety and stability.

REMEMBER If you get upset at any point while reading the handbook, or doing the exercises, STOP. Do something pleasurable and, when ready, resume the activity, or reading.

2 Understanding childhood sexual abuse

This section aims to give you a better understanding of childhood sexual abuse (CSA). It will therefore look at how CSA is defined, how common it is, who is most at risk and how abusers groom children. You may want to skip this section to continue to work through the handbook, and come back to it at a later point.

What is CSA?

As a survivor of CSA you may feel you know everything you need to know about CSA and do not need a definition. Or you may want a definition so that you can legitimise your sexually abusive experience. The current definition of CSA used by the Department of Health 2006 is:

'Forcing or enticing a child or young person to take part in sexual activities, including prostitution, whether or not the child is aware of what is happening. The activities may involve physical contact, including penetrative (e.g. rape, buggery or oral sex) or non-penetrative acts. They may include non-contact activities, such as involving children in looking at, or in the production of, sexual online images, watching sexual activities, or encouraging children to behave in sexually inappropriate ways.'

The spectrum of CSA

The spectrum of CSA is very broad and ranges from non-contact behaviours such as voyeurism and taking child abuse images, to contact behaviours such as oral and penetrative sex. Your experience can fall anywhere along this spectrum. The important issue is whether or not you had a choice and could give informed consent. CSA rarely happens in isolation but occurs alongside emotional abuse, physical abuse or neglect, and domestic abuse. It is usually repeated over many months or years, and can be committed by more than one person.

In essence, CSA is the systematic abuse of power and need to control which is channelled through sex. CSA also involves deception, the distortion of reality and dehumanisation of the child through the betrayal of trust. These all have a significant impact on the child and later adult.

The subtlety of CSA

It is unlikely that your CSA rarely started with an act of rape and that your abuser(s) may have spent considerable time grooming and manipulating you to gain your trust. You may have been made to feel special, enjoyed the extra attention or felt aroused by the sexual contact. Perhaps the abuser(s) made you believe that sexual contact between adults and children is a normal way to express love and affection for each other. Alternatively, the abuser(s) may have blamed you for the CSA making you believe that you wanted it and were the seductive one.

Such distortion of perception and reality will have made it harder to legitimise your experience as abusive. This is precisely what the abuser(s) hoped to achieve as it minimises the risk of disclosure and detection. Although you may find it hard to define your sexual experience as abusive or traumatising, this handbook can help you gain clarity and meaning.

How common is CSA?

Statistics on CSA vary enormously depending on the definition used and how the data was collected. It is generally agreed that approximately **one in four girls** and **one in six boys** experience CSA.

However as CSA is largely hidden, we can never be sure of how common CSA actually is. Many children and adult survivors never disclose their abuse which means that available statistics may only ever represent the tip of the iceberg. For instance, it is estimated that only one in nine cases of CSA are reported to the authorities, of which 10% of cases get to court, and only 10% of these result in a conviction.

In 2010 The NSPCC reported that there were 21,618 sex crimes against children recorded by police in England and Wales in 2008-2009 which represents an average of 60 sexual offences against children per day. Furthermore, one in seven children were below the age of 10, three out of four were 10 to 17 years old, and approximately 1,000 children were under the age of five. Girls were six times more likely to be abused than boys and the offender was four times more likely to be known to the child than a stranger.

Who is most at risk of CSA?

As can be seen from the NSPCC data, children of all ages are vulnerable to sexual abuse. CSA can happen to children across the whole social, economic, ethnic and religious spectrum. The risk is increased in children with disabilities or who have unstable home lives. Children who are in care or have been socially excluded are also at a higher risk, as are those who have unsafe immigration status or have been sexually trafficked.

Although all children are at risk of CSA, abusers often target vulnerable children as they are less likely to disclose, which reduces the likelihood of detection. Very young children who are pre-verbal are also at risk as they are unable to disclose the abuse. They are also more likely to normalise their experience as they have nothing else to compare it to.

Girls have been shown to be more vulnerable to CSA than boys. This may however not be the case in reality, as boys often find it harder to disclose abuse due to strong social barriers. Males are often raised to be strong and stoical in dealing with hurt and pain, and are thus discouraged from talking about such negative experiences.

Boys may be more vulnerable to CSA in certain contexts such as in clerical abuse. There is considerable evidence of large numbers of boys raped by priests or members of other religious faiths. Many of these boys, and later adult men, have been reluctant to disclose their abuse for fear of challenging the moral authority of the religious institution, and fears around their masculinity and sexuality.

Who are the abusers?

The majority of child sexual abusers are male, although it is estimated that around 15% to 20% are female. The taboo of CSA by females makes it much harder for children, or adult survivors, to disclose for fear of not being believed. In addition, CSA perpetrated by females may be more hidden as it is conducted under the pretext of personal hygiene, or loving and care-taking behaviours.

Perpetrators of CSA come from all age groups including children, adolescents and senior citizens. There is increasing awareness of CSA by children and adolescents with an estimated one third of all CSA committed by children and adolescents under 18 years of age. This includes older brothers or sisters, peers, school friends or neighbours. If you were sexually abused by an older child or adolescent you are more likely to believe this was consensual even if it wasn't. CSA can also occur across generations in which grandparents, parents, aunts, uncles and older siblings are all involved in the sexual abuse of a child.

Research has shown that 87% of abusers are known to their victim. These are usually members of the immediate or extended family, friends of the family, partners of the child's parent(s) or carer(s) as well as neighbours, teachers, nursery workers or child-minders, carers, tutors, sports coaches, youth leaders, priests and religious leaders. Professionals such as doctors, paediatricians and other respected members of the community are also known to sexually abuse children. This suggests that child sexual abusers come from all walks of life, ethnic origin, religious faiths, social economic backgrounds and class.

There is also evidence of ritual CSA in which a number of members of a community are involved. Your abuser(s) may have come from any one of these categories, or a number of other ones.

Paedophiles sexually abuse large numbers of children, sometimes as many as 250 children, before being detected. This has certainly been the case in clerical abuse where large numbers of children were abused over many years. To ensure access to and a constant supply of victims, many paedophiles deliberately choose careers that give them power and authority over children.

It is worth reflecting on your experiences to consider whether you were really able to give informed consent. Did the other person exploit your need to feel special, or lack of knowledge, for his or her own needs or for sexual gratification? It might help to read articles or books such as *The Seduction of Children* (Sanderson, 2004) which explain how abusers groom and manipulate children into believing that they want to have sexual contact.

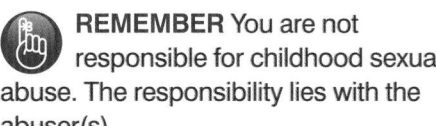 **REMEMBER** You are not responsible for childhood sexual abuse. The responsibility lies with the abuser(s).

The impact and long term effects

CSA impacts on the child and later adult in a number of significant ways. First and foremost, the abuser(s) has to dehumanise the child so that he or she becomes a sexual object to be used solely to satisfy the abusers sexual needs. Once the child has been turned into an object the abuser(s) can then impose whatever identity the abuser(s) wants to onto the child, such as temptress, whore or sex slave.

This false identity can stigmatise the child and evoke crippling shame and guilt. The distortion of perception and reality means that the child can no longer trust itself in its own experiencing. This is made worse if your body responded by becoming sexually aroused as you will no longer be able to trust your body, or feel that you have control over it. This leads to further shame, guilt and self-blame that you were responsible for the CSA.

In the words of one survivor: *'CSA is a mind f**k' in distorting all your thoughts, feelings and behaviour, in which black becomes white and right becomes* *wrong.'* The legacy of this is an inability to trust yourself, your mind or your body.

Disconnection from self and others

The betrayal of trust, confusion of painful feelings and the inability to trust in yourself can lead to a disconnection from yourself and others. This can lead to the avoidance of intimacy and relationships. In turn, withdrawal from others can lead to isolation and alienation.

Alternatively you might trust too easily and become over-intimate too quickly in the hope that someone will genuinely like or rescue you. To protect yourself in relationships you might resort to 'mind reading' in which you anticipate the feelings, thoughts and behaviour of others. As you disconnect from yourself you lose contact with your basic needs and how to express them.

Relationships

Instead you will become skilled at anticipating the needs of others and spend all your time trying to fulfil them, at considerable cost to yourself. As you become increasingly compliant and people pleasing you will consistently prioritise the needs of others over your own. You will also find it harder to assert yourself or say 'no'. This will make it hard for you to set boundaries around touch, personal space or emotional or psychological intrusion, which will make you vulnerable to further abuse.

Even if you believe that your CSA experience was conducted in a loving, caring or special relationship it can nevertheless be traumatising. The impact of CSA can lead to post traumatic stress reactions such as intrusive memories, nightmares and flashbacks (see **Managing flashbacks, nightmares, panic attacks and dissociation** on page 70). If you were drugged during your abuse by either rohypnol, ketamine, alcohol, sleeping tablets or formaldehyde in cigarettes, or were encouraged to use illegal drugs, your memories might be even less clear.

Coping strategies

To manage the impact of CSA you will have developed a number of coping strategies. Some of these will be highly adaptive at the time such as dissociation, avoidance of intimacy or withdrawal, while others are potentially self-destructive. You may have found that using substances such as drugs, alcohol or food helped you to regulate your mood, or block out terrifying feelings and memories. Or you may have resorted to other addictive behaviours such as gambling, shopping, sex or self-harm as a way to make you feel better or to cope.

Sexuality

CSA also impacts on your feelings of self-worth, relational worth and sexuality. This can lead to added confusion about your sexuality, sexual identity or sexual orientation. It may have left you feeling asexual or sexually dissatisfied. To cover this up, or to prove that you are desirable or lovable, you may have had periods of sexual promiscuity which have left you feeling more empty and disconnected. Alternatively you might have had other sexual difficulties such as compulsive masturbation, erectile difficulties or vaginal muscle tension which prevents penetration.

Loss of safety and hope

A further impact of CSA is to shatter your assumptions about others and the world as a benign place. If you see others and the world as unsafe it will prevent you from engaging with others or wanting to discover the world. CSA can also lead to a loss of hope in a better future. This loss of hope can have a huge impact as it leads to a sense of foreshortened future and loss of spirituality. If you were abused within a religious context it can lead to spiritual injury in which you lose your faith in God, or higher being, which is an important part of your identity. Loss of spiritual belief is often accompanied by a number of other losses, all of which will need to be grieved.

REMEMBER While CSA has a considerable impact on the child as well as the later adult, it is worth remembering that many of these difficulties can be worked through. This will lead to post traumatic growth in which hope and vitality are restored. The very fact that you are reading this book indicates that you have not lost hope, and that the warrior within is still very much alive. It is important to acknowledge and honour this as it will help you in your recovery. As you continue to work through the book and start to restore control you will find that CSA will no longer define you. You can begin to live more authentically by reconnecting to yourself, others and the world.

3 Understanding CSA and trauma

Trauma is usually defined as an overwhelming threat to life, serious injury or physical integrity involving intense fear, helplessness or horror. Trauma can consist of a single event or multiple and repeated traumatic events. Commonly CSA consists of a series of repeated traumatic experiences over prolonged periods of time, which usually involve multiple violations such as sexual assaults, physical violence, emotional abuse and neglect. To help you understand your reactions to trauma you will need to have some knowledge of how your body responds to trauma. This section therefore includes some scientific information which can appear quite complex to begin with. If you prefer, you can skip this section and return to it at a later point.

The impact of trauma

You may have been abused by a single abuser, or you may have suffered from systematic sexual abuse involving several perpetrators. The impact of trauma will vary from person to person and depend on the type of trauma, your age, the frequency and duration of the abuse, and your relationship to the abuser(s). What is common to all, is the physical and psychological reactions to trauma which serve to protect you. These reactions are like an **emotional immune system** which instead of fighting invading bacteria or viruses, fights to protect you from sexual, physical, emotional or psychological assault. In essence this is your warrior within.

Your emotional immune system

To help you cope with danger, and to aid survival, your brain releases a cascade of neuro-chemicals which start a complex chain of bodily reactions. These are designed to protect you from the harmful effects of the trauma and help you to survive. Your emotional immune system does not stop the emotional pain, stress or trauma from happening, but does cushion the trauma and helps you to deal with it.

Just like the physical immune system, the emotional immune system acts outside of conscious awareness and is therefore not under your control. It is vital to acknowledge that whatever your reactions during the trauma, these were outside your control and therefore you are not to blame or at fault for how you responded. Recognising this can dramatically reduce any crippling feelings of shame, self-blame or guilt.

REMEMBER Your reactions to trauma are outside your control and you are not to blame for how you responded during the CSA.

Your body's alarm system

In the presence of danger the body's **alarm system** is tripped and goes on red alert. Once on red alert the alarm system sends signals to the body to prepare for **fight, flight** or **freeze**. This sets off two crucial biological defence systems: the **sympathetic nervous system** and the **parasympathetic nervous systems**. The sympathetic nervous system mobilises high level energy necessary for fight or flight, while the parasympathetic nervous system slows down the heart and metabolic rate which results in the freeze response.

Your alarm system is regulated in an area of the brain called the **limbic system** by two structures: the **amygdala** and the **hippocampus**. The role of the amygdala is to detect threatening information through external senses such as touch, taste, sound, smell or vision. The amygdala is responsible for determining whether incoming stimuli is desirable, benign or dangerous. To maximise survival, this evaluation is instantaneous but crude and primitive in that it does not use deeper analysis, reason or common sense. This is why it is often referred to as the *'fast and dirty route.'*

If the stimulus is life threatening, stress hormones such as adrenaline and cortisol are released which send messages through the nervous system to the muscles and internal organs to either attack, run or play dead. The amygdala is highly sensitive to any danger and is easily activated to increase readiness to attack or defend (**fight**), run (**flight**) or submit (**freeze**).

In contrast to the 'fast and dirty' route of the amygdala, the hippocampus is a much slower route in that it evaluates the external threat through deeper analysis using conscious thought, memory, prior knowledge, reason and logic. The hippocampus is also critical in laying down new memories and experiences. If the danger is truly life threatening, the hippocampus will send messages to continue with appropriate responses. If however the deeper analysis concludes that the stimuli are not dangerous it will send messages to deactivate the responses. In most cases of threat these two structures work in harmony to balance appropriate responses to the situation.

Breakdown of the emotional immune system

In prolonged and repeated trauma such as in CSA, the feedback loop that controls these two systems malfunctions and floods the body with high levels of stress hormones. While these stress hormones are critical for survival, they are highly toxic and only designed to circulate for short periods of time so that you can get to a place of safety or remain safe until the threat is over. In the case of CSA where the child cannot fight or run to safety, the only option is to freeze. This means that the stress hormones cannot be discharged and remain in the system, which can have a number of negative consequences.

Evidence shows that high levels of cortisol that are not discharged can lead to the destruction of brain cells which can affect the function and size of the amygdala and hippocampus. Such malfunction leads to increased fear and anger responses, as well as memory impairments.

Alarm system default setting constantly 'on'

When the brain and body is flooded with chronic levels of stress hormones, the hippocampus goes 'offline' and is unable to accurately evaluate the degree of threat or danger. It is also not able to assess whether the danger is internal or external, or whether the traumatic incident is over or ongoing. As a result it cannot send the appropriate messages to the amygdala to deactivate the alarm system. This leads to the alarm being on constant red alert and the continuous release of stress hormones.

This means that your body will continue to respond as though the trauma is ongoing, even after the threat or sexual assault is over. As the alarm remains on a default setting of 'on', you will feel and act as though you are being repeatedly traumatised. This leads to a heightened or continuous state of danger, known as **hyper-arousal**. This hyper-arousal forces stress hormones to continue to flood the body and brain, which results in the tyranny of post-traumatic stress responses.

Storing new memories

As the hippocampus can no longer regulate the alarm setting, or halt the release of chronic levels of stress hormones, its ability to store new memories is reduced. This means that the trauma is not stored within context or time, making it seem as though it is continuous and never ending. This in turn prevents the processing of the trauma keeping it 'online' with the same vividness and intensity as when the actual assault happened.

Not being able to process the experience will make it harder for you to store it in memory or recall it (see **Managing memories** on page 80). This leads to incomplete or fragmented memories, or a lack of memory of the experience. It is for this reason that recovery from the trauma of CSA must include bringing the hippocampus back 'online'. In doing this, its function will be restored so that it can regulate your alarm system, accurately evaluate danger, and differentiate between internal and external threat.

Damage to physical well being

High levels of circulating stress hormones can also impact on your physical well-being leading to hypertension, physical exhaustion, chronic fatigue syndrome (CFS), sleep problems, or digestive, respiratory and endocrine problems. In addition, chronic fear reactions and high levels of adrenaline can result in tsunami like anger which you cannot express for fear of consequences. This means you have to push your anger down thereby creating even further stress. Hyper-arousal also affects your concentration and the processing of information, making it hard to gain meaning from your experience, or how it has impacted on you.

The role of the freeze response

While the emotional immune system activates three alternative reactions, fight, flight or freeze, in most cases of CSA there is only one option – to freeze. The freeze response is designed to conserve energy so that you can escape when the danger is over. As young child you cannot out run or fight an adult effectively, so you are left with no choice but to freeze. While the freeze response protects you from the greater threat of the consequences of fighting back or running away, it can feel like passive submission. This can make you feel as though you were weak in not fighting back, or running away, which can lead to self-blame and guilt.

In reality, a child can never fully escape especially if the abuser(s) is a significant figure in the child's life such as a parent, relative or priest. In that moment you are both powerless and helpless. However, the sense of submission can often haunt you and leave you feeling ashamed that you did not do more to prevent the sexual assault.

The freeze response is also designed to protect you from the full impact of the pain of the sexual assault. As the parasympathetic nervous system kicks in, a sense of calmness descends on the brain, slowing everything down, and the body begins to feel numb to cushion the anticipated pain and the emotional terror of the sexual assault. Once the danger is over, these reactions fade and you can discharge the stress hormones through movement.

In CSA and repeated traumatic experiences in which there is no escape, these hormones are not discharged and continue to circulate leading to increased numbness, paralysis, dissociation, psychological deadness or collapse. Thus the terror and distress do not go away but tend to grow stronger over time, causing even more intense distress which the mind tries to block through avoidance or numbing.

REMEMBER Freezing is NOT giving up or a passive act of submission. It protects you from further harm and is not a conscious choice but part of the alarm system when in danger with no means of escape.

Post-traumatic stress disorder

About a third of survivors of CSA develop symptoms of post traumatic stress disorder (PTSD) or more often complex PTSD. The most common PTSD symptoms are divided into the following three categories.

Post-traumatic stress disorder symptoms

1 Persistent re-experiencing of the trauma such as recurrent and intrusive memories, recurrent distressing dreams or nightmares, reliving of the traumatic experience through flashbacks, intense psychological distress and to internal or external cues that resemble the trauma, and physiological reactivity to internal or external cues reminiscent of the trauma.

2 Persistent avoidance of stimuli associated with the trauma, and numbing of responsiveness as seen in avoidance of thoughts, feelings, activities, places and people associated with the trauma, inability to recall aspects of the trauma, diminished interest in activities, feeling detached and estranged from others, restricted range of feelings, or emotional anaesthesia and sense of foreshortened future.

3 Persistent symptoms of increased arousal such as difficulty falling or staying asleep, irritability or outbursts of anger, difficulty concentrating, hyper-vigilance and exaggerated startle response.

Persistent re-experiencing of the trauma can be triggered by both internal and external cues. This means that even if you are not in actual external danger, feelings and sensations experienced on the inside can trigger a range of PTSD reactions. Given that you may already be in a high state of anxiety, it is easy to set off an already highly sensitive alarm system on the basis of internal physiological arousal.

This can be potentially dangerous as you may not be in touch with external reality and therefore cannot judge the degree of danger objectively which means that actual danger is not recognised, and safety cannot be acknowledged. Some survivors can go on to develop complex PTSD.

Complex PTSD

In the case of complex PTSD the symptoms become chronic as they begin to affect the very core of the self. Complex PTSD is commonly seen in people who have experienced prolonged sexual or physical abuse, or torture. Like PTSD, complex PTSD results in hyper-arousal, and strong out-of-control physiological reactions. It also impacts on how you think about yourself and others, how you feel about your body and how you relate to others. In addition, complex PTSD can result in the distortion of reality, stigmatisation and a deep sense of shame. To manage such strong reactions can lead to an avoidance of all feelings, even pleasurable ones, and a withdrawal from others leading to social isolation. In order to avoid shame, you may retreat from the world and feel as though you are living your life in a bubble.

PTSD and complex PTSD can produce a range of other psychological effects and disorders, especially anxiety disorders such as **agoraphobia** and **social phobia**, **depression**, **obsessive compulsive disorder**, **borderline personality disorder** and **chronic fatigue syndrome**. It can also give rise to a number of physical complaints such as **headaches**, **irritable bowel syndrome** and **unexplainable aches and pains**, which are your body's way of expressing emotional distress.

To regulate out of control emotions and trauma reactions you may resort to self-injury or self-medication through food, alcohol or substance misuse, sex addiction or gambling. You may use such behaviours to dissociate, or to either numb or release the emotional or psychological pain. Whichever methods you use to regulate your pain, these are commonly accompanied by chronic feelings of ineffectiveness, shame, despair or hopelessness and feeling permanently damaged. In addition, distorted perceptions result in negative thoughts such as self- blame, as well as loss of previously valued beliefs. The loss of trust in others can lead to defensive tactics such as avoidance or hostility, and a lack of trust in a safe or benign world.

Distortion of reality

CSA and trauma can also disrupt the natural regulation of sensory perception whereby internal and external reality is so distorted that you are fooled into thinking that danger is present when it is not and vice versa. As your reactions to trauma seem beyond your control, you may feel betrayed by your body making it even harder to trust yourself or your reality. This lack of trust reinforces your need to avoid feelings and people which further increases the sense of alienation from self and others. An important part of your recovery will be to restore your reality through more accurate sensory perception and interpretation. This will allow you to gain a better balance between your internal subjective reality and external objective reality.

Remember that your external reality is monitored by your sensory system using sight, sound, smell, touch and taste. In contrast, your internal reality is monitored by sensations such as heartbeat, pulse rate, muscle tension and breathing. It is also dependent on your **proprioception** which is how you sense your body's location in space. The distortion of external and internal reality is most noticeable when the abuser(s) makes you feel special, or tells you that what is happening is pleasurable despite feeling ashamed. This can cause tremendous confusion especially when what is happening to you is unpleasant or shameful, and yet your body responds with sexual pleasure.

Such distortion of reality can lead you to believe that CSA is normal or that it has had no harmful or damaging effects on you. If you believe this, it is likely that your abuser(s) deliberately distorted your reality by normalising the abuse, or by performing sexual acts that you experienced as pleasurable. This will have minimised your perception of the traumatising effects of CSA making it harder to legitimise it as abuse.

 REMEMBER Even if the CSA was subtle and non-violent, it **can still be traumatising in distorting your reality and overall sense of confusion.**

To manage the effects of CSA and trauma it is necessary to restore control over your bodily reactions and trauma symptoms, and reset your alarm system. This can be achieved through a variety of techniques which you will find in part two (see **Managing your reactions to trauma** on page 54).

4 Understanding your reactions to CSA and trauma

As CSA and trauma impacts differently on each individual it might be helpful to reflect on how it has affected you. To get the most from this section, you may wish to read only what applies to you and skip those that do not apply. Prior to making that decision it is worth considering the following exercise.

EXERCISE Make some time for yourself free of any interruption to write an account of the whole of your CSA experience(s) in your journal. This can be done over several days and remember to stop if it becomes too distressing. Write down everything that happened, what were you doing, thinking and feeling in the present tense. Make sure to include your reactions, physical sensations and all you saw, smelled, heard, touched or sensed around you, as well as what it meant to you. Highlight what was the worst for you and how your experiences changed you, and how the trauma continues to impact on your life now. Allow yourself to experience any feelings and sensations without judging them. On a separate page list your reactions to the trauma and identify any PTSD symptoms. Remember to reward yourself when you have completed this exercise.

In looking at this list how do you think you have coped with your traumatic experiences? What are your main reactions? Are you plagued by re-experiencing or reliving the experiences through intrusive memories, nightmares or flashbacks? Do you tend to avoid anything associated with the traumatic experiences? Do you tend to dissociate and tune out, or withdraw into yourself and isolate yourself from others? Do you feel empty, or emotionally dead? Do you mainly live in your head? Do you still feel that you live in a war zone and live in constant state of red alert, or **hyper-arousal**, with out of control feelings? Do you find yourself unable to concentrate or sleep? Do you find yourself in a high state of watchfulness, or **hyper-vigilance**, in which you can never relax? Or are you frequently unaware of your surroundings, **or hypo-vigilant**?

Remember these are all normal reactions to trauma, and these symptoms helped you to survive. They may seem crazy making and frightening but they do have an adaptive function and make sense. For instance hyper-vigilance ensures that you are alert in a hostile world, while dissociation anaesthetises the psychological pain making it easier to survive emotionally. While these reactions have helped you in the past, this has been at a cost to you in not being able to regulate your mood. As a result you are plagued by out of control feelings, anxiety, suicidal thoughts or destructive behaviour such as self-injury. To soothe these you may use drugs, alcohol or food as a form of **self-medication**. To gain some control over your responses it helps to have a deeper understanding of the impact of post-traumatic stress reactions.

Hyper-arousal

Hyper-arousal, a classic post-traumatic stress reaction, is when you are in a constant of high alert due to the increased levels of stress hormones such as adrenaline and cortisol flooding your body. This results in feelings of restlessness, anxiety, irritability or out of control emotions. High levels of adrenaline lead to physiological responses such as elevated heart rate, palpitations and sweating. It also increases feelings of uncontrollable anger or rage, and wild mood swings. As your nervous system becomes overloaded with stress hormones you sway between high levels of agitation and total exhaustion.

As your default setting is on high alert, all your energy and resources are diverted to managing your stress reactions and survival. This means it is harder to think clearly, evaluate external or internal cues accurately, or make sense of your experience. In essence you are unable to use your 'brake' to regulate your reactions making it difficult to gain control over your body, thoughts or feelings.

Lack of control

As your physiological reactions take on a life of their own, you feel less able to control them. Even more distressing, this can also happen when you have pleasurable experiences. For example, excitement, physical exercise or sex have similar internal sensations such as increased heart rate and breathing, sweating and muscle tension as your fear responses, and therefore can trip your alarm system. This means even pleasurable feelings or activities are experienced as dangerous thereby reducing your ability to enjoy life.

Hyper-arousal can also disrupt your sleep, rest and eating patterns. At times you may be so stressed that you simply cannot eat or sleep, let alone rest. This can cause further problems as your body is not able to recuperate through rest, which can result in exhaustion and chronic fatigue. Hyper-arousal can become such a normal state that you may have no conscious awareness of its effect on you, its origins or its link to abuse.

Knowing the origins of your hyper-arousal, and recognising it is not you going 'crazy', is the first step in taking control. It is vital to release the trapped energy and discharge the high levels of stress hormones so that your body can rest and reset your alarm system. **Managing sensations and feelings** on page 63 looks at how you can release stress hormones in a healthy way, through movement and exercise, to allow you to take more control over your post traumatic reactions.

Hyper-vigilance

Hyper-vigilance, which is a symptom of hyper-arousal, also makes it hard for you to relax or let your guard down. As you are constantly anticipating threat you are on high alert as you monitor your environment for any signs of danger. This is seen in an increased **startle-response** in which you jump at any loud noise or stimuli, and are in a constant state of watchfulness. In contrast, you might be so preoccupied by your internal sensations that you 'tune out' from your environment, and become **hypo-vigilant**. This puts you at risk of threat as you are not aware of actual dangers in your surroundings.

Avoidance

One way of managing trauma is through avoidance. This can include avoidance of trauma cues, people, places or activities associated with the trauma including intimacy and sexual relationships. All of these can lead to social isolation and deep sense of aloneness. Alternatively, you may avoid feelings and thoughts through numbing or dissociation as a form of anaesthesia. Or you might avoid feelings and thoughts through sleep, watching endless television, relentless work schedules or keeping yourself busy at all times.

This is a way to escape, distract or block any distressing feelings. You might also avoid feeling through the soothing or numbing effects of food, alcohol, drugs or self-injury. While these provide short term relief, avoidance actually intensifies negative feelings and thoughts. Every time these are avoided they become 'stamped in' as they remain unprocessed and un-integrated.

Post-traumatic stress reactions

Post-traumatic stress reactions are largely due to avoidance or lack of emotional processing which means they are not fully integrated. There is considerable evidence which shows that when people avoid feelings or thoughts, these will intensify and be twice as likely to recur, generating even more distress.

Flashbacks

Flashbacks are another common post-traumatic stress reaction. Flashbacks are very intense and vivid recollections of traumatic experiences that have not been fully processed and integrated into your memory system. As they are so intense they can activate the same cascade of bio-chemicals and stress hormones as the original trauma thereby mimicking the real thing. This sets off similar bodily reactions such as pounding heart, changes in breathing, sweating and muscle tension designed to fight or flee. As you have the flashback your body may begin to take on the same postures and survival mechanism you did as a child such as cowering, freezing, submission or playing dead. To help you manage flashbacks more effectively see **Managing flashbacks, nightmares, panic attacks and dissociation** on page 70.

REMEMBER Flashbacks are normal reactions to traumatic experiences and they do not mean that you are going 'crazy'.

It is critical that you acknowledge that you are NOT being abused again, but that the flashback is a memory of something that happened in the past. In effect it is a flash 'back' to a previous experience, which due to its intensity fools the mind and body into feeling and believing that the past event is happening now in real time. Flashbacks can represent a single past event, or encapsulate a series of traumatic incidents.

Flashbacks can be triggered in a number of ways. It could be because you are in the presence of actual threat in the environment, or by internal bodily sensations which are similar to when you were in danger in the past. Alternatively, a range of sensory stimuli such as images, sight, sound, smell, taste, touch or the position of your body that are associated with CSA can also trigger flashbacks. They can also be triggered by certain actions, intentions or emotions reminiscent of the trauma or certain words, places, objects or by someone who resembles your abuser(s). If you are currently experiencing trauma, or struggling with loss, this can also ignite flashbacks.

Nightmares and vivid dreams

Nightmares and vivid dreams are a common after effect of trauma and an important part of the survival system. In essence nightmares are the night time equivalent of flashbacks and therefore represent unprocessed aspects of the traumatic experience. Nightmares also symbolise emotional aspects of the trauma such as feelings of shame, humiliation and anger. Like flashbacks, dreams and nightmares help you to sort through your experiences in order to file them away in your memory bank, albeit while you are asleep rather than awake. You may find that your nightmares are more terrifying than flashbacks. This is because while you are asleep your resources and coping strategies are 'off line' making it harder to manage them.

If nightmares and dreams remain unprocessed they will keep recurring, making you fearful of going to bed, or finding it hard to go to sleep. If you are able to fall asleep, and have the nightmare, your sleep will be interrupted and you will have difficulties falling asleep again. Such interrupted sleep will leave you feeling tired and exhausted when you get up. When nightmares occur several times per night, every night your energy levels and resilience will be eroded making it extremely hard to function during the day. If left unresolved, the lack of rest and sleep can make you vulnerable to chronic fatigue syndrome.

TOP TIP To help you manage your nightmares and dreams keep a dream diary so that you can process them and improve your sleep patterns.

If you suffer from recurring nightmares see **Managing flashbacks, nightmares, panic attacks and dissociation** on page 70 and **Managing memories** on page 80 to find ways of managing nightmares and how to process traumatic memories more effectively.

Panic attacks

Panic attacks are characterised by a sudden surge of intense anxiety and are often due to prolonged periods of stress. They can be triggered by something specific that is frightening, or more often they will occur spontaneously for no apparent reason. As they can happen any time, they can prevent you from going out or tolerating situations in which the panic attack first occurred. The fear of having a panic attack can lead to social withdrawal and anxiety, and fear of leaving the house, or **agoraphobia**.

Signs of panic attacks include shortness and shallowness of breath, pounding and irregular heartbeat, a sense of feeling 'unreal' pains or tightness in chest similar to heart attack, unsteadiness, trembling and dizziness, and the feeling that the world is spinning around. You may also experience excessive sweating, feeling faint and light headed, a fear of losing control,

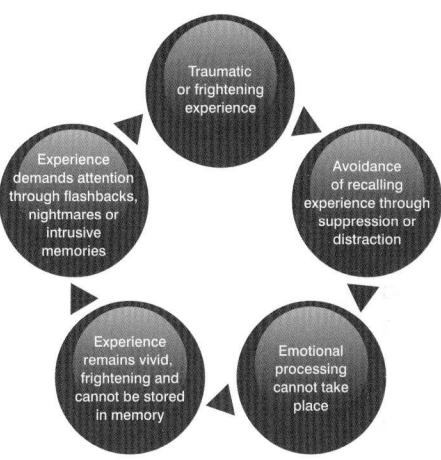

Figure 1 How traumatic experiences become intrusive memories

going crazy or even dying. This is often accompanied by tingling in the hands and feet, choking or feeling you are being smothered, flushed skin, urgent intense need to run away, nausea and a powerful urge to scream. The intensity of the symptoms can make you feel as though you are having a heart attack. To help you manage your panic attacks, see **Managing flashbacks, nightmares, panic attacks and dissociation** on page 70.

Intrusive memories

To understand intrusive memories it helps to understand the role of memory to survival. Memory is a necessary aid to survival as it stores both positive and negative experiences. Positive or pleasurable experiences are stored so that they are repeated while negative or unpleasant experiences are stored so that they can be avoided. Memory is very complex and dynamic. It is not static like a video recording, but constantly adds and subtracts when integrating new experiences into past experiences.

In essence, we process experiences by reviewing them, elaborating them and linking them to other experiences. This then allows them to be stored as memories in order to direct future behaviour. In addition, as you process experiences you will be able to make them less frightening by reducing their emotional intensity. To use a computer metaphor, it's a bit like saving your document in a folder to be accessed when you need to, rather than not saving the document at all so it stays 'on line' waiting for your attention every time you go to your computer.

REMEMBER Unprocessed experiences are harder to store in memory because they are still 'alive', demanding constant attention. This means they will remain as frightening as when you first experienced them.

Figure 1 above left illustrates how this occurs. Traumatic experiences are usually triggered by sensory cues such as sounds, smells, the feel or taste of something, being touched or certain words. These demand attention through the feeling of intrusive memories.

Intrusive memories are so distressing that you will try to avoid them, not realising that this makes them even more vivid and frightening, and twice as likely to recur. The more you try not to think about them, the more they will spontaneously recur and demand your attention. Rather than process them you might try to block them out through dissociation, the use of alcohol, drugs, food or self-injury. Alternatively, you might try to distract yourself by thinking of something else, keeping busy, working or not talking about it.

Dissociation is often referred to as 'mental flight when physical flight is not possible' and is a highly adaptive response to inescapable trauma such as CSA. It provides a 'mental shield' to allow you to detach from feelings, bodily sensations and reality. The signs of dissociation include feeling spaced out, or being in a dazed or dreamlike state. Your attention is more narrowly focused as you tune or screen out the world around you.

You might find that means your external world appears unreal or surreal, in which time has slowed down or speeded up, or in which familiar places, people or objects seem alien or appear not to exist, known as **derealisation**. You may be plagued by unusual body sensations as if floating away, looking at yourself from a distance or that your body is split off from other parts.

As you split off from your body, it seems like experiences are not happening to you but to someone else. As you are out of contact with your body and not processing your experiences, there will be huge gaps in your memory, or complete amnesia of the trauma. As your mind unconsciously blanks out part or all of the memory you lose a sense of continuity of who you are and your reality, known as **depersonalisation**.

⚠️ **WARNING** **To ensure your safety while dissociating, do not drive or operate machinery. Make sure young children, pets or any dependents are safe.**

Everyday dissociation

Everyone dissociates to some degree whether through daydreaming, being on autopilot or detaching from different aspects of experiences. This can be seen when 'tuning out' while reading a good book, gardening, watching a film or when listening to music. These are all normal and healthy forms of detaching from reality, but you can also detach through less healthy behaviours, such as alcohol or drug misuse, binge eating or self-injury, which can put you at further risk of harm.

Dangers of dissociation

While dissociation is a normal response to trauma, it can impact on everyday functioning. You may become so out of contact with your body that you constantly live in your head and lose contact with all inner sensations. Or you may also armour your body to such an extent that you have no awareness of your feelings or powerful internal signals that can tell you that something is not right. Another danger of sealing off your feelings, is that others may experience you as cold and unfeeling which reduces opportunities for intimacy in caring or loving relationships.

If you 'tune out' too much you will lose contact with your surroundings and can no longer monitor threat or danger. Alternatively, if you dissociate during an experience you will have no recollection of what happened. While this emotional anaesthesia initially aids survival, over time it can result in changes in your sense of self, in your body, your sense of reality, time and memory.

Frequent detachment from your bodily experiences gives rise to a loss of reality and uncertainty about whether the experience happened to you or someone else. This unreality about your body and self can result in you feeling like a shadow of a person, rather than a real human being. You may also find yourself dissociating from pleasurable experiences leading to emotional and psychological deadness or frozenness in which you feel nothing at all. Moreover, dissociation requires huge mental energy which is both physically and mentally exhausting and draining.

Finally, dissociation can put you at risk as you are less able to monitor potential external danger in your surroundings. If you have children, pets or dependents you can put them at risk by not being able to protect them while you are in a dissociative state. In addition, as dissociation is an avoidance strategy it prevents you processing your experiences, thereby increasing the need to dissociate which can interfere with your recovery.

Dissociative identity disorder

Under certain circumstances, frequent and continuous dissociation can result in such fragmentation that several separate personalities are formed to support the person. This is known as **dissociative identity disorder** (formerly known as **multiple personality disorder**) wherein you are no longer a single functioning personality, but are inhabited by a number of other distinct personalities. Such severe dissociation can interfere with your everyday functioning and you are urged to seek professional help. For help with managing dissociation and becoming more embodied see **Managing flashbacks, nightmares, panic attacks and dissociation** on page 70.

WARNING Although dissociation is a normal response to trauma it can interfere with your everyday functioning. If you are concerned, it is vital to seek professional help.

5 Understanding the process of recovery and healing

The process of recovery

The process of recovery is unique to each survivor and varies from person to person. The journey can be gruelling at times with stops and starts, with massive obstacles or blockades, or detours and diversions, as well as miraculous breakthroughs. You will also find that it is made up of a continuous chain of small achievements rather than big leaps. To restore control and take charge of your life and future requires patience, stamina, hope and commitment. One way to help you take ownership of your recovery is to create a metaphor or symbol that represents your healing process.

Metaphor

To help you capture the process of recovery it helps to find a **metaphor** or **symbol** that illustrates how you see your recovery, including obstacles and setbacks as well as progress. You could use an actual journey that consists of both difficult terrain and diversions as well as clear, straight roads. The metaphor that works best for you will be one that reflects your interest or hobby such as playing a musical instrument, managing a sports team, repairing or building something, or tidying up an overstuffed cupboard. Or you could use the image of the warrior within that has protected and fought for you so far, or the analogy of nurturing your inner child.

TOP TIP Find a metaphor that illustrates your healing process and use this to prepare for your journey to recovery.

Some survivors find a gardening metaphor useful as it includes a number of factors needed for growth. For example light, nutrients in the soil, fertiliser, regular watering and protection from extreme weather. To truly thrive and flourish the garden needs regular attention through adequate drainage, watering and feeding, as well as weeding and pruning to maintain the best environment for quality growth.

EXERCISE Reflect on what metaphor is most useful for you and write this down in your journal. Try to focus on the role of commitment, dedication and practice, setting goals and achievements as well as pitfalls and setbacks. Remember to consider the feeling of triumph and growth that you will have at the end of your recovery and include that in your metaphor. Your metaphor not only prepares you for the hazards and delights of your journey, but will also help you when you feel discouraged during the process of your recovery.

Your inner strengths and resources

Before embarking on your journey you need to be prepared for any potential hazards and ensure that safety structures are in place. To help you in this it is important to identify and recognise your existing strengths and resources that have helped you to survive so far.

EXERCISE Identify what has helped you to get this far including your strengths, inner resources and coping strategies. Effectively call forth your warrior within and list how he or she has fought to protect you. As you list your strengths and resources in your journal make sure that you celebrate these. Next, review your list and consider how you can build upon these and what can help you in that.

TOP TIP Identify your warrior within by making a list of your strengths and resources that have helped you to survive.

To aid your recovery you will need to make sure that have a good support network of people you can trust. This can include family or friends, as well as a professional such as your counsellor or key worker. You can also extend your support network to include other survivors by joining a support group. Make a note of the contact details of everyone in your support network and make sure you speak to at least one person for at least five minutes every day. If you can't meet up then make sure you phone, text or email them daily.

Regaining control

To aid your recovery and allow you to come out of survival mode you will need to regain control over any traumatic reactions and symptoms. Research has found that control and a sense of purpose are the two most positive factors in recovery from trauma. Regaining control over distressing and overwhelming reactions allows you to process feelings and experiences which will help you to take charge of your current everyday life. It will also enable you to manage stress, restore healthy sleeping and eating patterns, and generally improve your quality of life.

To help you to restore control see **Restoring control and grounding techniques** on page 55 and **Managing sensations and feelings** on page 63. Make sure that you practice grounding techniques on a daily basis so that you gain mastery over them. You can also take control by creating a sense of achievement, even in such routine tasks as ironing or tidying up. You can do this by injecting fun and pleasure into them such as listening and dancing to your favourite music while performing these mundane tasks.

TOP TIP The most positive factors in recovery from trauma are control and a sense of purpose.

Sense of purpose

Your commitment to your recovery will give you a powerful sense of purpose which is the second most important factor in recovery from trauma. Remember the focus and primary purpose in your recovery is you and improving the quality of your life. This sense of purpose will restore meaning to your life and allow you to live more honestly with a greater sense of vitality. Central to this is the setting of personally meaningful goals that are realistic, achievable and measurable. To maximise achieving your goals it is important to check that they will not be hampered by such restrictions as time, money and access to resources.

EXERCISE In your journal list your personally meaningful goals for recovery and rank these in order of priority with the most urgent at the top and the less urgent at the bottom. Highlight those goals that you want to focus on immediately and rank these in order of importance. Starting with the most important, identify all the steps that are needed to attain this goal. Highlight the steps you have already taken and list those you need to take next to achieve the goal. Once you have identified your goals you need to reduce these down into small manageable steps and ask yourself what step you can take today to achieve your goal. At your own pace, work through each step until you achieve your goal. Remember to validate each step that you accomplish and keep a record of your achievements to chart and monitor your progress.

To reach your goals you might need to experiment with different ways of achieving each step and your ultimate goal. For example if you are afraid to sleep in the dark, put a light on. If you are afraid to sleep in the bedroom allow yourself to sleep on the sofa. Take your time and try different methods so that you find the right steps to reach your goal.

REMEMBER If a task is too difficult or upsetting, stop, take a break from it and make a commitment to return to it at a later point.

Pacing yourself

It is crucial that you do not rush your recovery and that you go at your own pace. To help you pace yourself it is important to break down the process of recovery into small manageable steps. This allows you to practice new ways of being, and to think about your accomplishments. It is important that you savour your achievements and take pleasure in your accomplishments. In doing this you are more able to see that goals are attainable which gives you the courage to continue.

Avoid rushing

It is important not to rush your recovery as rushing increases the likelihood of setbacks. For example, you may want to be hugged, but if this is still too overwhelming you may dissociate which will make you even more anxious and fearful of being hugged. This will set you back rather than help you to move forward. In addition, rushing may be reminiscent of the abuse experience. To get through the sexual abuse you may have 'rushed' through the experience in order not to feel or be upset. Rushing your recovery will mean that you will not process your experience of healing and find it harder to value your achievements.

Slowing down also reduces trauma cues and gives the mind and body time to embed new ways of being. It is much better to start slowly and consolidate each step than to leap forward only to stumble backwards or relapse. You might find slowing down frustrating at times but it is worth persevering as you are more likely to achieve and ensure a better guarantee for future success.

REMEMBER Go at your OWN pace as this is the one that gets you to your goal in a time frame that is right for you. Do not allow anyone to rush you.

Rewarding yourself

Central to your recovery is celebrating your achievements. This is crucial in validating your courage, and in restoring self-confidence and self-esteem. It also reminds you of your sense of purpose and your progress. A good way of rewarding yourself as you achieve your goal is to make a 'cookie jar'.

EXERCISE To make a 'cookie jar', write down positive things about yourself on small strips of paper. These could include your positive qualities, compliments people have paid you or your accomplishments and achievements. Find a nice jar or container, or customise an old jam jar.

Next roll each strip into a ball and place inside your 'cookie jar'. Whenever you want to reward yourself, or remind yourself of positive things in your life, take out a ball of paper and read out loud what it says.

💡 **TOP TIP** It is important to reward yourself as you achieve your goals. Try making a 'cookie jar'.

Coming out of survival mode

Regaining control, finding a sense of purpose and valuing your achievements will help you to come out of survival mode. While you are in survival mode you are constantly alert to danger, and will tend to focus exclusively on potential threat and negative aspects in your world. This leaves no energy or mental space to notice positive things in your life. As you begin to feel more in control and move from survival mode to feeling more alive, you can begin to incorporate more of the positive aspects of the external world. Gradually this will allow you to balance negative feelings and experiences with positive ones. While this will not cancel out the negative, or undo your experiences, it will create a better balance. Such balance opens up opportunities to make meaningful choices rather than being controlled by negative thoughts, feelings or abuse experiences.

REMEMBER When you are in the middle of feeling low you cannot focus on positive things.

As you recover you will free up trapped energy and notice the difference between surviving and living mode. This extra energy will enable you to engage in more pleasurable activities that are nurturing and growth promoting. As you experience more positive things in your life, the quality of your life will start to improve allowing you to live your life as you want to live it.

Changing cues from the past

To aid your recovery you need to counterbalance traumatic experiences by reintroducing pleasure into your life. A good starting point is to replace the negative cues present during your abuse with more positive ones. For example, if the abuse took place indoors, in a darkened room then make sure you keep curtains and windows open to let light and air into your room. If your abuse took place in silence, then have music playing or have the radio or television on. In the case of unpleasant smells replace these with pleasant ones such as scented candles or incense. If you were abused in a clerical context beware as incense could trigger negative memories.

EXERCISE Changing sensory cues – reflect on your abuse experience and try to identify as many cues associated with the abuse. For example did the abuse occur indoors, at home or other premises such as church, youth club or outside in a car, tent or field? List some of the most powerful cues such as whether it was light or dark, quiet or noisy, cold or warm, tidy or messy? Also try to recall any smells associated with the abuse and your ability to breathe. For instance, if you were restrained or pinned down during the abuse this would have restricted your breathing. Try to link these cues to how they affect your mood and sense of well-being. As you do this begin to list opposite sensory cues, and experiment with these. For example, if you felt unable to breathe see how it feels to open the windows and allow fresh air to circulate. Notice and record any changes in how you breathe, and how it feels to inhale fresh air rather than stale air, and how this affects your well-being and mood.

Changing sensory cues from the past can seem unfamiliar and strange at first but it is worth trying to change as many of the negative cues that you can so that there are less reminders of the abuse to haunt you. As you replace negative sensory cues with more positive ones you will find that your sense of well-being will improve. You will also find that you will want more positive experiences in your life.

Reclaiming pleasure

Letting go of negative cues from the past allows you to seek out more enjoyable activities that give pleasure and meaning to your life. For instance, if you felt silenced as a child then sing, shout or scream. If you were constrained then move around, dance or swim. If you were prevented from playing find a hobby that allows you to play, or spend time with friends in fun activities. Or if you were isolated you will want to seek out and develop friendships. If you find it hard to trust people then find other sources of trust such as animals or nature.

EXERCISE In your journal make a list of pleasurable activities you enjoy including good people you like to be around. Also list the treats that you find positively rewarding and nurturing. Try to include calming and soothing as well as invigorating and stimulating activities, alongside inspirational and creative ones. You could also reclaim a hobby or passion you had in childhood and pursue this again. Make a commitment to build these into your weekly schedule of self-care.

💡 **TOP TIP** Singing, talking and writing is a way of reclaiming your voice while smiling and laughing is a way of reconnecting with others.

Living in the present

The more you engage in pleasurable activities the more you will override your negative childhood experiences and live in the present. Try to simplify your life by refining routine chores, making these more fun and reducing your work load and commitments. This means learning to set boundaries and being able to say 'no' without feeling guilty. Remember your goal is to reclaim pleasure without guilt or fear of it being wrenched away. You can maximise this by performing daily positive acts such as smiling, singing or being in contact with trusted friends.

Gradually you will achieve increasingly longer periods of calm and contentment. This will make it easier to manage the difficult times with more energy, vitality and renewed optimism. You will be able to enjoy living in the present rather than being catapulted into your past, which will lead to greater stability and contentment.

Renewed energy

As you become less haunted by the past and feel less threatened and controlled by it, you will be able to release trapped energy in your body. This renewed energy can now be directed towards enjoyable physical activity such as dancing, swimming, walking or other forms of exercise. This can renew vitality which helps you to wake up with enthusiasm for the day ahead rather than dreading it. It will also allow you to become more relaxed and empowered rather than being flooded with fear and anxiety.

Reclaiming yourself

Recovery from CSA is not just about reclaiming yourself, it is also about building a more complete person for the life that you want. It is about writing your own life script rather than have someone dictate and control it. A useful metaphor to illustrate this is likening your life to a book. While the early part of your life, or chapters, were directed and written by someone else, such as your abuser, future chapters will now be written by you. You can control whether to throw away earlier chapters, rewrite new ones or build on earlier chapters by changing the course of future chapters. With you as author you have complete control over changes that you want to make and how to live the rest of your life.

REMEMBER The past no longer needs to dictate the present and how you are. You can now choose pleasurable and positive experiences that enliven you and bring you joy.

While you cannot undo what the abuser(s) has done to you, you can reclaim who you are and create your present and your future in the absence of abuse.

EXERCISE To help you reclaim yourself, list how your life would have been if you hadn't been abused. What were your hopes, dreams, goals, values? Remember these were stolen from you and can be reclaimed. Look at this list and compare it with your goals for recovery and see how they compare. Make a second list, in order of importance, of what you wish to reclaim and the steps needed to achieve these.

Reclaiming yourself will promote a more positive focus for your future as it will allow for post-traumatic growth, and a return of vitality and spirituality. You will be able to reconnect to yourself, others and the world. Letting positive things into your life will help you in taking care of and nurturing yourself.

Reclaiming positive aspects of your life

In reclaiming positive aspects of your life you need to identify all the things that you have in your life for which you are grateful. This will form the basis of your '**gratitude journal**'. Research has shown that keeping a 'gratitude journal' can improve happiness and satisfaction. It also enables you to make a conscious effort to 'savour' all the beauty and pleasure in your daily life no matter how small.

EXERCISE To write a 'gratitude journal', divide a section in your journal, or find a new small notebook in which to record all the things in your life for which you are grateful. This could include your health, your children, your friends, your family, your pet(s) as well as the things you appreciate in life such as nature. To help you try to become more conscious of the good things in your life. Make time to listen to the sound of birdsong or the rustle of leaves, to notice the shimmer of sunshine or autumn leaves turning into riot of colour, or breathe in the tang in the air. You could also consider writing a gratitude letter to someone important in your life, past or present, even if not alive, that you have never properly thanked.

Becoming more consciously aware of the good things in your life not only helps you to stay in the present, but remind you that you are a part of something bigger. This can go a long way of making you feel good about being alive. Allowing positive things into your life will not take away or make up for the CSA, but it will re-balance your life.

Keeping a weekly record of all the good things in your life and your achievements will provide evidence of your recovery and post-traumatic growth. Along with gratitude and humility it will make you more appreciative of your life which will help you to manage setbacks. And while you may not be 100% free of trauma reminders, your recovery and growth will help you to bounce more quickly and allow you to feel thankful for the gift of life.

TOP TIP Every day before going to sleep recount three good things that have happened that day.

6 Understanding obstacles to recovery

Although recovery is liberating and empowering it is also scary. Change can be very stressful and stir up powerful emotions. While this is normal, you will need to be prepared for this and check whether you are ready to take on additional stress.

Before embarking on your journey to recovery it is important to ensure that your support network is in place and you have a degree of stabilisation. This will help you manage any obstacles on the way. Obstacles are a normal part of the recovery process and are primarily opportunities for growth. If you can embrace these opportunities for growth you will be less likely to fear that your journey will be in vain. Like the flower that closes at night for protection but opens the next day in all its glory, your recovery must include protection and willingness to risk opening up.

REMEMBER The circle of life is characterised by change and rebirth in which growth becomes more vigorous and resplendent.

Change is difficult

Change is always difficult as it is hard to give up habits and old patterns of thinking and behaviour. As habits they have become conditioned and deeply ingrained making it harder to imagine alternative ways of being. Your reactions become automatic and seem to occur outside any conscious awareness. This is because your reactions are frozen in time and will need to thaw. As you gradually acclimatise to change and reduce your fear, you will be able to reduce the obstacles to your recovery.

Many of the obstacles to recovery stem from the fear and stress of change. Each person will have specific anxieties and concerns that are unique to them. Some will welcome the opportunity for change, while others are terrified. It is normal to have mixed feelings about change and it is helpful to acknowledge these.

EXERCISE To identify your fears around recovery and change, make a list of all your worries and anxieties. These may centre on re-experiencing the trauma, increased emotional distress, increased need to self-medicate or the impact change might have on your relationships. Next make a list of how you numb your thoughts and emotions, such as food, alcohol or drugs, and link these to potential obstacles to your recovery. Once you have identified some of the obstacles, reflect on how you can overcome them. It also helps to discuss your concerns with a trusted friend to help you develop a plan of action to manage any obstacles.

Overwhelming feelings as an obstacle

A common obstacle to change is that it will stir up overwhelming emotions which feel unmanageable. Your fear will set off your alarm system making you even more anxious. As your focus shifts onto your internal sate of anxiety you will be unable to balance this with your external reality. To manage these fears you might resort to old patterns of avoidance or emotional numbing through the use of alcohol, drugs, food, work, sex or self-injury. A return to self-medication will inevitably create obstacles to emotional processing and hijack the recovery process.

 **TOP TIP** Identifying your fears is the first step to overcoming them.

Fear of regressing

Fear of regressing is a further obstacle especially if there is an increase in trauma reminders and symptoms. This can also trip your alarm making change seem too difficult as the fear of re-traumatisation will outweigh any gains of recovery. This could lead to increased fear of failure and doubts about ever getting better as the damage is so great.

Such a spiral of fear is a good reason not to seek quick, radical changes but to savour and value each small step and achievement. Change which is more gradual and less noticeable will seem less fearful and be a more solid foundation for recovery.

Fears and anxieties

Fears and anxieties can stop you from thinking and reduce your ability to make decisions. This can create further obstacles which will interfere with plans for change and recovery. You will need to calm and sooth these anxieties so that you free up mental space and energy to think clearly. The clearer your thinking the more you will be able to make informed choices rather than activating automatic defensive reactions.

Self-fulfilling prophecies

Your fears can lead to self-fulfilling prophecies. An illustrative example is a fear of not having a healthy relationship, or having children. This fear can be so paralysing that you avoid all opportunities to have a relationship just so that you can avoid this dilemma. Underlying self-fulfilling prophecies is jumping to conclusions and projecting into the future. In order to prepare yourself for your worst fear you predict it will happen so that you can 'psych' yourself up for the worst case scenario. This can create significant obstacles to your healing.

Secondary traumas

Another common stumbling block is the fear of secondary traumas linked to CSA. You may fear that you have sustained irreparable physical damage, and therefore can't have children, or that your sexuality has been affected and will never find a partner. Or you may have an aching feeling of emptiness and loneliness that can never be soothed, or a constant fear of abandonment. Or you may fear your neediness or dependency. All of these can lead to obstacles in your recovery. It is important to recognise that all of these can be worked through and overcome.

Trauma reactions such as flashbacks, nightmares and intrusive memories can lead to exhaustion and lack of energy which can present further obstacles to your recovery. To minimise this try to improve your pattern of rest, work and play, and take regular exercise. It is also useful to regulate eating patterns, and improve your diet. To increase your energy levels it helps to reduce your caffeine, alcohol and sugar intake. This will help you to restore zest and vitality to your life which can help you to overcome any obstacles to change.

Feelings of anger

Feelings of anger can also become a stumbling block especially if it has been suppressed over many years and involves a range of people. You may feel angry with your abuser, your non-abusing parent(s), your family, or social services, the church or the criminal justice system. Such powerful unexpressed anger can become all consuming and prevent recovery. While such anger is natural especially if the abuser(s) has not been held accountable it can become toxic. Intense, unexpressed anger can be hard to let go and prevent you from moving forward.

If unexpressed anger is dominating your life you will need to find healthy ways of releasing this in a safe and secure environment, preferably with someone who can contain it such as a counsellor or therapist. Releasing this anger is the first step in letting it go, so that it no longer infects your life and allows you to move forward.

Shame and guilt

Shame and guilt can also create obstacles to your recovery especially if you blame yourself for the abuse (see

Managing shame, guilt and self-blame on page 99). Blame prevents you from legitimising CSA and leaves you feeling responsible for your abuse. This is particularly the case when there has been a lack of recognition of CSA from others such as the abuser(s), family, friends or the criminal justice system. Self-blame reinforces your feelings of shame as you falsely believe that you enticed or encouraged the abuser(s).

A further source of shame is if you experienced pleasurable sensations during the sexual abuse, or sought contact with the abuser(s). It is critical that you understand that pleasurable sensations during sexual contact are normal and do not mean that you wanted the sexual abuse. Similarly, seeking contact with your abuser(s), on whom you are dependent, is not evidence that you wanted or encouraged sexual abuse. Obstacles that derive from self-blame, shame and secrecy can seem insurmountable and yet can be worked through (see **Managing shame, guilt and self-blame** on page 99).

Lack of self-worth

A related obstacle is stigmatisation and believing that you are 'damaged goods'. This leads to a false belief that you do not deserve, or are not entitled to, better treatment or better life. This can result in a crippling lack of self-worth which prevents you from being assertive or asking for your needs to be met. Becoming over identified with being a victim who has no voice or rights can lead to further negative self-beliefs which will undermine your recovery.

Your critical voice

The lack of self-worth is often supported by negative and critical self-talk in which you constantly put yourself down. This can sabotage your recovery, as such negative inner dialogue affects not only your self-esteem but also your mood. Such critical messages act as internal saboteurs which become major obstacles to change and recovery.

EXERCISE To identify and change your critical voice and the impact of negative self-talk, list all the negative messages you tell yourself. Next state one of these and be mindful of any sensations or emotions that arise in response to this critical statement. Next, say something positive or comforting and reflect on how that feels. If there is a noticeable difference, try to balance or override negative self-talk with positive self-talk to fully aid recovery. For help in identifying negative self-talk and how to replace these with more positive messages see **Managing negative thoughts and negative beliefs** on page 88.

Current unhealthy relationships are often the most resistant obstacles. If you are in an unhealthy or abusive relationship you feel fear upsetting the other person for fear of rejection or abandonment. As unhealthy relationships are primarily conditional, you will fear losing them if you begin to express the full range of your feelings and thoughts. This fear of abandonment or rejection becomes a powerful motivator to not make changes even if your relationships are unhealthy.

REMEMBER Partners, friends and family may feel threatened by your recovery as this can reduce their power over you.

This is made worse if you feel you do not deserve, or are not entitled to, empathic understanding or to be supported when trying to make changes. This can be further complicated if partners and friends may have a vested interest in you not making changes, especially if this threatens to reduce the power they have over you. Such partners or friends will not want you to change as you will be less easily manipulated, or if it means you will become less compliant, or dependent on them. The more your partner or friend feels threatened by your recovery the more they will sabotage any changes you make. In combination, this can undermine recovery and prevent you from becoming free from the past.

Gains and losses of change

Recovery and change can generate both gains and losses, and it is critical that you are aware of this so that potential losses do not become major obstacles. To prevent this it is better to be prepared for any losses so that you can make informed choices as to which changes you can realistically make, at a pace that suits you.

 EXERCISE In your journal draw two columns, one headed *'What I have to gain'* the other *'What I have to lose'*. Under each heading, list all relevant gains and losses in your recovery. Seeing these written down will enable you to clearly see why the process of recovery is so hard. It will also allow you to make realistic commitments to your recovery. Review the two lists and think about what resources are available to help you tolerate losses and changes.

Reducing obstacles to recovery and change

Reducing obstacles to recovery and change means you need to pace yourself. Rushing can undermine recovery as you leap forward only to retreat back. Remember recovery takes time and slowing down allows you to consolidate change. By accepting a slower pace and not berating yourself that you are not moving forwards fast enough will remove one of the major obstacles. It is also normal to become despondent, or lose your faith in yourself at times. Accepting this rather than fighting it will be more beneficial. Do not allow loss of hope to become an obstacle by ensuring that you keep faith in your warrior within. Keep your inspirational anchors nearby to remind you that you can have a better quality of life and that it is possible to recover.

REMEMBER The willingness to believe that change can occur and that experiences, emotions and thoughts are not set in stone but are dynamic will help you to embrace change.

Finally, be mindful that the journey to recovery is not a straight line and that is normal to encounter obstacles that force you to backtrack or make detours. There will be relapses which fuel despondency and can undermine your faith, hope and resolve. See **Preventing relapse** on page 142 for help you if you do have setbacks.

The essential thing is to recognise that relapses and obstacles are part of the process and that these provide endless opportunities for discovery and learning. It is important to keep your faith and have the confidence to find your way back to your chosen path rather than abandon the journey altogether.

Part two
Managing your reactions to trauma

7 Restoring control and grounding techniques

Loss of control

A significant impact of CSA is the loss of control. This includes loss of control over your feelings, your thoughts and your body as well as your actions and behaviour. In addition control over your autonomy and reality is reduced. Lack of control over these essential functions ultimately decreases your capacity to live your life to the full and make informed choices. A central aspect of recovery is to regain control over your physical and emotional responses to CSA.

To gain control and mastery over CSA, and to overcome the tyranny of trauma reactions, it is vital to reset your inner alarm system. This means making sure that the default setting is changed, and that your alarm is not so easily tripped. This will allow the hippocampus to come back online to restore physical and emotional balance.

To achieve this renewed control it is helpful to find ways of reducing your daily stress levels, stabilise your trauma reactions and restore a sense of inner safety.

Reducing stress

One way of achieving greater control over the quality of your life is to reduce daily stress levels by simplifying your life. It is essential to have some structure to your life to counteract the chaos associated with CSA trauma. This can be done by ensuring regular routines and rituals around going to bed, eating of meals, taking exercise and resting. Streamlining daily routines and rituals will help you to be more organised and give a structure to your daily life.

Routines do not have to be boring

Routines create safety, balance and an element of control, as long as you don't overdo it! The aim is to reduce stress in the here and now in order to make your trauma reactions more manageable. You can make routines more fun by listening to loud, invigorating music when you are cleaning, ironing or washing the dishes. To further tame your day to day stress levels it is essential to set boundaries, and not take on additional responsibilities or demands. This means learning to say 'no' and not feel guilty.

Restoring control over your eating and sleeping patterns

Another way to take control over your life is to ensure that you restore control over your eating and sleeping patterns. Eating regular, healthy meals can counter stress reactions and regulate your bodily functions. If you have suffered prolonged traumatic stress reactions it might be worth taking vitamin supplements such as vitamin B and vitamin C, which are often depleted during stress. Increasing your intake of Omega-3 can also help to lower stress levels. Discuss this with your GP so that you can replenish any vitamin deficiencies and restore your energy levels.

The role of sleep and rest

A healthy balance between sleep, work, rest and play helps to restore out of control stress levels. Sleep is essential to rest the body and to aid the processing of emotional experiences. It is also critical in the formation, storage and consolidation of memories. Sleep is also necessary for inspiration and finding creative solutions to everyday problems. If you are plagued by nightmares and find it hard to get to sleep, you will need to experiment with a range of strategies that help you to sleep – see **Managing flashbacks, nightmares, panic attacks and dissociation** on page 70. Regular bedtimes and regular waking times, as well as relaxation exercises, can all aid sleep.

Physical exercise

Physical exercise is especially important if you adopted a freeze response during CSA, or find it hard to relax. Relaxing can feel like giving up control and submitting, as you had to during the abuse, and can make you feel even more vulnerable. If you find it hard to relax, or if relaxation increases your anxiety, then physical exercise may be a better choice for you. In contrast to relaxation, physical exercise involves tensing your muscles to give you a sense of being in control and in charge of your body.

Both relaxation and physical exercise can help you to reconnect to your body, which is vital if you have become detached and out of contact with your body. Restoring control over the body is particularly important if you felt betrayed by your body in responding to the CSA. It is essential that you find what is best for you to remain in contact with, and in control of, your body.

Releasing stress hormones

Physical exercise is an excellent way to stay in the present, or here and now, rather than focusing on the past. It is also a powerful antidote to the freeze response in discharging trapped energy, which sends messages to the brain to switch off the alarm system as the trauma is finally over. Not only do you discharge trapped energy, but you also release built up stress hormones such as adrenaline and cortisol which have grown to toxic levels. As the built up stress hormones fade away you will find renewed levels of energy to regulate current stress levels.

Increased muscle tone

As the stress hormones are released and you exercise with new vitality you will discover a sense of well-being as feel-good hormones, known as **endorphins** are released into the brain. A further benefit of physical exercise is the increase in muscle tone. Research has shown that increased muscle tone is a much more powerful ally in trauma than relaxation, as it makes you physically stronger which in turn promotes greater emotional strength. Physical exercise also encourages you to breathe and to regulate your breathing, which is another aid to reconnecting to and restoring control over your body.

As the freeze response prevents the discharge of trapped energy, the body remains frozen. If you want to start exercising it is better to thaw your frozen body slowly by engaging in gentle exercise. If you do this too quickly you can cause further damage so it is better to start gradually and build up slowly. Moving the body slowly through carefully chosen exercise can cancel out the paralysing effects of CSA and help you to regain control over your body. As you begin to feel your body move and shed its protective armour, you can build up to more strenuous exercise.

 WARNING Before engaging in regular physical exercise you need to have a medical check-up with your GP or the practice nurse, especially if you have taken no exercise for some years.

Regaining contact with your body

Physical exercise not only allows you to release trapped energy and shed its protective armour, it also allows you to regain contact with your body, allowing you to become in tune with your body. This means you will feel your body more, known as **embodiment**, and be able to live in your body rather than trying to escape from it. This will reduce your body shame, while increasing your capacity to contain arousal and stress responses.

Increasing your sense of body protection

To enable you to feel more embodied start by becoming more aware of your body by moving whenever you feel yourself detaching from your body. Start gently by wiggling your fingers or toes, moving your arms or legs, rotating your head or standing up. Gentle muscle tensing in the legs, feet and back can also have beneficial effects. These activities can give you improved balance and a sense of being grounded, while strengthening your body and increasing your sense of protection.

Remember your body is a powerful resource as it provides important signals about your inner experiencing. As this has been largely terrifying in the past you have shut down these signals. While this has felt like shrouding yourself in protective armour, it has put you at greater risk. Physical exercise can help by sending messages to the alarm system that the trauma is over and that you no longer need to freeze. As your body thaws and your armour melts away, you will become more in tune with your body and bodily signals. This will help you to truly protect yourself and strengthen your bodily responses.

WARNING Strenuous physical exercise might not suit you as increased heart rate, respiration and sweating can mimic the arousal during the sexual abuse. If this happens, you will need to find lower levels of activity that do not increase heart rate or respiration such as slow weight training, muscle tensing, swimming or gardening. Remember to experiment to find what works of you. To help you choose which forms of exercise appeal to you the most, try the exercise below.

EXERCISE In your journal list any physical exercise that appeals to you. A selection of options could include walking, jogging, step classes, bicycling, weights, sit ups, push ups, ball games, pilates, yoga, treadmill, swimming, tennis, golf, self defence, boxing, kick boxing, martial arts, tai chi, riding, gardening or dancing. Highlight those that appeal to you and that you would like to experiment with. Make a commitment to try one at a time and be mindful of which is best for you. It is worth trying out some slow, gentle exercise as well as some fast, high paced exercise to see how you feel both during and afterwards.

Before you make your decision, check how realistic your chosen physical exercise is. How much time can you realistically commit in terms of the frequency and duration of the physical exercise. It is also important to consider any financial costs such as class fees, gym membership and ease of access to the location. You also need to consider whether you prefer outdoor or indoor activities, or prefer to exercise at home.

If you are socially isolated you may consider pursuing group activities or team sports, or finding an 'exercise buddy' to keep you motivated. When you have tried a few alternatives, settle on those that have been the most effective for you and that you can realistically manage. Remember you are trying to reduce stress rather than increase it! Finally, it might help initially to reward yourself every time you take exercise to sustain your level of motivation. For example, you could put some money into a box every time you exercise.

 REMEMBER Strenuous exercise which increases heart rate and respiration can mimic the arousal during sexual abuse which can trigger trauma reactions.

Mindfulness

To support greater awareness and control over your body and physical being, it is useful to develop mental strategies that track your sensations, emotions, thoughts and feelings. You can achieve this through **mindfulness** which helps you to become more consciously aware of your current thoughts, feelings and surroundings. As well as increasing awareness of your experiencing, mindfulness encourages you to accept such experiencing without judgement. This helps you to keep an open channel of communication between your mind and body. As you develop this you will become more aware of how your mind and body are linked and your experiencing.

Mindfulness will also help you to monitor the impact certain foods and drinks have on you and your body. For instance, caffeine tends to increase physical and psychological tension, known as **hyperarousal**, whereas carbohydrates have a calming effect. This is useful to know so that you can regulate your body by being more mindful of what you eat and drink. Test this out by monitoring your reactions to caffeine and carbohydrates in a more conscious way.

Becoming more aware of the impact of what you read or see, either on television or in films, or hear, such as music, or topics of conversation, through mindfulness can also help to regulate such stimuli. If your alarm system is already on high alert, or you find it hard to filter incoming stimuli, you will benefit from finding ways of reducing sensory overload. Try to find regular time to sit in quiet surroundings so that you can just focus on you and your experiencing.

Identifying triggers

Mindfulness can also help you to identify the triggers that cause intrusive memories, flashbacks, dissociation or panic attacks. In identifying these you will be able to understand which triggers you are sensitised to. This will help you to prepare for anticipated problematic reactions, as being forewarned means you are forearmed. To help you with this try the exercise below.

EXERCISE To identify triggers, look at your list of trauma reactions and try to identify as many triggers as you can that trip your alarm system. Do not worry if you can only identify a few. As you work through your traumatic reactions using mindfulness skills you will be able to identify more triggers which can be added to the list. Next try to grade the triggers on a scale of one to four, with **one** being triggers that are the least difficult to manage; **two** being triggers that you are not able to cope with yet but may be able to handle soon; **three** being triggers that are hard to control but you would like to master in the future; and **four** being those triggers that you will always wish to avoid for your own or others safety. Starting with those triggers that are least difficult to manage write down what happens and how you would like to control these, and how this can be achieved.

Grounding techniques

One way of restoring control over triggers and traumatic reactions is to find **grounding techniques** that will allow you to stay connected to yourself and your current reality. Grounding techniques will also remind you that you are safe and no longer in danger. Grounding techniques are particularly useful to manage anxiety, intrusive memories, flashbacks, dissociation, panic attacks and self-injury.

Using all your senses

The most effective way to ground yourself is to connect to all five senses: sight, sound, touch, smell and taste preferably with objects that represent your current reality. Thus it is better to focus on objects and stimuli in the present rather than the past. To make grounding techniques work for you, you need to personalise them by making them specific to you. You will also need to practice and rehearse these techniques so that they become familiar and automatic.

The first step in grounding yourself is to refocus your attention to the present by concentrating on things around you. In this, you will need to focus on the physical space you are in and try to identify and name out loud as many objects around you.

You will already have identified some grounding techniques such as your anchor, oases and safe place. To these you can add your **grounding smell** such as a comforting or favourite scent or aftershave sprayed onto a scarf or fabric, smelling comforting spices such as vanilla or cinnamon, or a lavender bag or scented candle. Alternatively you could use stimulating smells such as lemon zest or pepper.

You could also add **grounding images** to ground you. If possible, try to make this image interactive. For example you could use an image of a secluded garden and make it interactive by walking around it. As you stroll around, smell and name each flower out loud, listen to the fountain and touch the leaves and grass. Alternatively you could create a luxury home and imagine yourself walking from room to room touching and naming all the beautiful objects you have. Or you could use a luxury car and imagine looking at and touching the interior, as well as the engine. The more pleasant the images are, the easier it will be to recall the images. You can support your image by collecting relevant pictures from magazines or vivid drawings that can be put into an album or collage. Remember to practice your grounding images daily so that they become automatic and can easily be recalled when you are in crisis.

Bridging image

To help you get to your grounding image or safe place, you need to create a **bridging image**. For example your bridging image could involve imagining yourself floating away from the trauma or traumatic reaction to your safe place. Imagine a trusted friend taking you there, or a door opening to reveal your safe place.

Grounding phrases

You could support your bridging image with a **grounding phrase** such as *'I am OK'* or *'I am strong, I have survived. I am safe'*. Remember to personalise this phrase using your own unique voice. To help you remember your grounding phrase you could send yourself a voice message and store it on your mobile phone. Alternatively, write it on a sticky note and stick it somewhere where you can see it. An elaboration of this could be identifying a **grounding song** that symbolises your survival or courage which you can play and sing along to.

Grounding body position

It is also helpful to find a comforting or **grounding body position** in which you feel safe and strong. This could be curling up in a comforting position with a favourite blanket, or standing up straight and tall with shoulders back to make you feel strong and powerful. Or you could tense your muscles and feel your strength course through your body. Experiment with a number of positions to find which is the most comforting or empowering for you and practice this whenever you can. Controlling your body in this way can be an effective way to regulate your mood as well as remaining embodied.

Grounding hobby

Finally, you could consider finding a **grounding hobby** in which you can immerse yourself such as painting, playing a musical instrument, doing a crossword or suduko, or collecting something meaningful to you. This will not only absorb you until the traumatic reaction subsides but it can also restore pleasure and fun into your daily life.

With your arsenal of grounding techniques you will further equip the warrior within to help you to face your triggers without detaching or engaging in self-destructive behaviours. This will allow you to move from avoidance which gives you the illusion of control, to truly being in control of your trauma reactions. Your grounding techniques will also help you to **regulate** your mood and emotional distress and allow you to confront the unprocessed aspects of your trauma. Remember the more you avoid the traumatic experience the more intense your emotional distress, and the more likely you are to re-experience the trauma.

Feeling more in control

Regulating your emotions will help you to feel more in control of them, This will also aid you in finding more healthy alternatives to manage trauma reactions (see **Managing sensations and feelings** on page 63). Physical exercise and grounding techniques will not only soothe you, but also help you reconnect to your body and to yourself. This will reduce your reliance on external sources of comfort such as food, alcohol, drugs or other people to regulate your emotional distress. You will find this extremely liberating as you learn that by trusting yourself you can take direct control over your responses and quality of life.

> **REMEMBER** In CSA someone else controlled you, your body, thoughts, feelings and behaviour, as well as your reality preventing you from acting autonomously. To recover it is vital to restore control to you so that you can choose what is right for you.

8 Managing sensations and feelings

To manage uncontrollable reactions and trauma symptoms it is vital to work through unprocessed experiences and emotions. The avoidance of distressing sensations and feelings results in a vicious cycle. The emotional content of flashbacks, nightmares and intrusive memories are pushed out of conscious awareness, or **suppressed**, and remain as raw as when first experienced. As they are not processed they are twice as likely to recur and re-emerge with greater intensity and vividness.

REMEMBER Avoiding or suppressing traumatic experiences means they are twice as likely that they will recur with greater intensity and vividness

Understanding emotions

To end this vicious cycle and to prevent more severe intrusive reactions it is vital that these traumatic experiences are attended to and fully processed. To help you in emotional processing it is useful to consider the benefits of emotions. Emotions are primarily signals and communications about experiences which provide a rich data base about you as a person. They are an essential part of you that help you to know and understand yourself.

Listening to your emotions

Listening to your emotions means that you have access to vital information that can guide you to make the right decision for you. You do NOT have to act upon them. In addition, suppressing your emotions requires considerable psychological energy. This causes considerable pressure which can be reduced once the emotions have been worked through and thereby improve your quality of life.

TOP TIP Feelings are valuable signals that you need to attend and listen to. They are not facts and do NOT have to be acted upon.

Emotional processing

Emotional processing allows you to balance your emotions and gain harmony rather than struggling to control your feelings through avoidance. It is vital to remember that feelings ebb and flow and do calm down. Your fear might be that once intense feelings have been activated they will not subside naturally but become constant and threaten to overwhelm you. To control this you will try to block them out, or push them down, preventing emotional processing.

It is essential that you restore the natural balance and ebb and flow of feelings. By interrupting this flow you have become out of contact with the natural, biological regulation of emotions. Recognising that feelings can be rebalanced naturally will help you to work in harmony with the flow of feelings rather than against it.

 REMEMBER Feelings and emotions ebb and flow and do subside.

An additional benefit of being in harmony with your emotions is that you will be able to appreciate your positive emotions more. In allowing this you will bring more spontaneity, richness and colour into your emotional experiencing. Listening to your emotions will enable you to draw on a much more powerful database of feelings to give you much clearer information about your experience.

Balance and harmony

This allows you greater balance and harmony rather than swinging between extremes, either not feeling at all or being flooded with tsunami like emotions. This can improve the functioning of your emotional immune system. Letting your emotions find their own balance without needing to be controlled allows you to be more in touch with your needs, and to express these. In being more open to your emotions, rather than being scared of them, you will find it easier to share them with others and improve the quality of your relationships.

 TOP TIP Emotional processing can improve your psychological and physical health as the internal battles subside and the balance of your emotional immune system is restored.

Processing your emotional traumatic experiences will let you absorb them rather than being plagued by them. This will allow you to restore your quality of life and take pleasure in everyday activities without being disrupted by overwhelming trauma reactions. Emotional processing will strengthen your ability to cope with other problems and enable you to develop creative, new solutions and ways of being.

Emotional processing style

We each have a unique emotional processing style, irrespective of whether we have experienced trauma. Your emotional processing style is a combination of learnt behaviour from your parents and family, your beliefs and attitudes, your temperament and predominant cultural norms. If your emotional processing is primarily as a result of learnt behaviour it is important to understand that learnt behaviour can be unlearnt. Knowing this offers you a choice over which style of emotional processing will be more beneficial to you in the future. This can help you to change those strategies that are no longer useful for your survival.

The most common emotional processing styles associated with trauma are **suppression** in which feelings are over-controlled and banished from conscious awareness; **avoidance** where emotions are avoided leading to unprocessed emotions and trauma symptoms; **over-reactivity** in which emotions and their expression are so overwhelming that they cannot be controlled; and **dissociation** in which emotions are blocked, cut off or compartmentalised.

The overwhelming nature of trauma and CSA increases the need to control emotions and avoid emotional processing. This leads to becoming out of touch or 'out of tune' with your emotions. The following exercise will help you to identify your **emotional processing style**.

 EXERCISE To identify your emotional processing style, think of your most frequent positive or pleasant emotions, and your most frequent negative or unpleasant emotions. Write these down and reflect on how you deal with such emotions. Is there a difference between how you manage pleasant and unpleasant emotions? Do you avoid unpleasant feelings? Do you tend to keep quiet about your feelings? Do you push your emotions away? Do you seal your emotions away so they cannot be accessed? How long do your emotions last – minutes, hours, days? How often do you feel the same emotions? Do you have difficulty controlling what you say when you are upset? Do you react out of proportion to what people say or do?

In answering these questions and exploring how you deal with emotions you identify your emotional processing style. As you identify your style ask yourself if you would like to change this and how you do this. To aid your recovery you might want to become more in tune with your emotions rather than avoid them.

Being in tune with your emotions

To help you become more in tune with your emotions you will need to attend and listen to them. This will help you to measure your sensations and feelings without becoming overwhelmed. To do this you must ensure that you have practised some of the grounding techniques introduced in the previous section (see **Restoring control and grounding techniques** on page 55). This is crucial as it will help you to regulate your emotional reactions if they threaten to overwhelm you.

Attunement

Becoming more in touch with your emotions promotes what is known as **attunement**. Attunement encourages you to notice and attend to your emotions on a moment by moment basis, and to value these as a rich source of self-knowledge. As you become more aware of your feelings you will be able to gauge the full range of your emotions and be able to manage these more effectively.

WARNING Do not attempt emotional processing until you have mastered grounding and breathing techniques, and gained confidence in using them to soothe and calm you.

Breathing

To help you restore control and to soothe and calm you, it is important to be able to breathe effectively. A common response to anxiety and fear is to breathe too quickly or shallowly. As we take in less oxygen the body begins to panic. This trips the alarm system, which heightens physical and psychological arousal and fear responses. The lack of oxygen also causes dizziness and shakiness which only serves to increase your panic.

An antidote to fear and panic is to breathe more slowly and more deeply to increase the intake of oxygen. Learning to breathe deeply will help to soothe and calm your fear and panic responses.

EXERCISE To improve your breathing you need to breathe slowly and deeply down into your diaphragm. It will help if you put your hand on your diaphragm, which is just above your navel, so that as you breathe your hand is pushed up and down. Count to five as you breathe in and five as you breathe out. Repeat this five times holding each breath for three counts. Monitor how you feel when you breathe more deeply and to what extent it calms and soothes you. Practise this until you feel confident in breathing more deeply.

In the case of panic attacks, or if you are hyperventilating, you will need to breathe very slowly and steadily and count along with each breath. If this does not work then you may need to use a paper bag. Take a paper bag and hold it over your nose and mouth tightly with cupped hands. This helps you to inhale the carbon dioxide in your breath which will help slow your breathing.

Bodily sensations

Once you have mastered grounding techniques and deep breathing the alarm system can be reset and you can begin to reconnect to your body. This will allow you to become more aware of bodily sensations. It is important to remember that your bodily sensations are a rich source of information about your internal state which helps you to identify internal cues more accurately. In restoring normal emotional functioning you will be able to monitor internal signals more objectively, and prevent internal stimuli overriding current external reality.

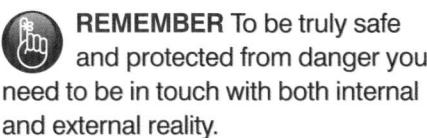

REMEMBER To be truly safe and protected from danger you need to be in touch with both internal and external reality.

Discriminating between bodily sensations

Being more in touch with your emotions also allows you to differentiate between sensations of trauma and pleasure. Sensations of fear and pleasure share similar aspects of physical arousal which can cause confusion in people whose emotional processing has been hijacked.

For example, accelerated heart rate is seen in fear as well as excitement and physical exertion. Many survivors associate increased heart rate with danger and fear as it is a reminder of the traumatic experience. As a result, many survivors of CSA are unable to experience or tolerate pleasurable sensation in their body. This can lead some survivors to actively avoid positive feelings or pleasure as they are associated with, and experienced as, traumatic fear responses.

Tolerating pleasurable sensations

As you become more able to discriminate between bodily sensations you will be able to tolerate, and feel more comfortable with pleasurable sensations.

This means you can allow your body to become a source of pleasure rather than plagued by panic and pain. It will also allow you to enjoy a full range of body experiences including relaxation.

Some survivors fear relaxation as it means letting down their guard and becoming less hypervigilant, making them feel more vulnerable and anxious.

If you find relaxation induces fear, panic, nausea or disorientation then it is not for you, and you may find muscle tensing more beneficial (see **Increasing your sense of body protection** on page 57).

Regulating your emotions

Resetting the alarm and gaining more control of your bodily sensations and physical and psychological arousal will help you to regulate your emotions. This can be achieved by gauging the intensity of your feelings and making sure you do not let them spiral out of control by breathing to calm you, or using the grounding techniques that work best for you. As soon as you feel your emotions rise, imagine plotting their intensity on a scale of one to ten, with ten being extremely intense. Once the emotional intensity rises above five you will need to practice breathing or grounding techniques to bring it down to a more manageable level. Remember it is easier to soothe and calm yourself if the intensity is at five rather than ten.

💡 **TOP TIP** To regulate your emotions imagine plotting their intensity on a scale of one to ten and as you feel them rise, try to lower their intensity through breathing and grounding techniques.

Regulating your emotions will allow you to move from avoiding feelings and traumatic reactions to tolerating distress as you feel more confident in regaining control. Breathing more slowly and deeply will help to ground you which will further enable you to tolerate arousal without being overwhelmed. In combination, this will permit processing of traumatic experiences and the release of suppressed emotions.

Releasing emotions

Releasing emotions, especially intense ones like anger, can be terrifying as they threaten to overwhelm. With increased emotional regulation you will be able to release trapped emotions more easily and effectively. This can be achieved by channelling their release more specifically through physical activities such as martial arts, tai chi, kick boxing, playing tennis, squash, jogging, riding a bike or swimming.

Alternatively they can be discharged by listening to invigorating music, drumming, dancing, vigorous cleaning, throwing bottles into a bottle bank, tearing newspaper, punching or screaming into a pillow or cushion.

You may prefer a less physical form of release by imagining your abuser(s) on an empty chair and telling him or her how you feel about what was done to you. Alternatively, you might prefer to write a letter to the abuser(s) describing how you feel about what happened to you and how it has affected your life. This letter is for your eyes only, or to share with a trusted friend, rather than for sending. It is designed to release your emotions rather than an actual confrontation.

Use whatever expressive words of anger, hurt, pain or confusion that come up. Do not worry about your choice of words, spelling or grammar, or how you construct your sentences. This is about committing words to paper, making your feelings more concrete and releasing the range of emotions you feel. You could write the letter from the perspective of both you as the child being abused, and you as an adult now.

This will give you as the child the voice you never had and enable you to express the anger and hurt that had to be suppressed. Notice how you feel at the end of writing the letter(s) until your anger subsides or is fully released.

WARNING Do not post any letters you write.

Expressing feelings

Identifying and acknowledging your feelings is the first step in emotional processing. Being able to tolerate them without being overwhelmed, knowing that they can be controlled and regulated will enable you to discharge them safely. Releasing suppressed and trapped emotions that have become toxic can be extremely liberating, as it frees up psychological and physical energy to tackle other difficulties that you might be facing. It will also help you to express your feelings in a more effective way.

Ultimately processing and expressing feelings will help to reset your alarm system. This will allow you to be more in control, to reconnect to your body and experience the full range of emotions including pleasure, joy and happiness.

REMEMBER The important thing is to find a method that works for you that helps you to tolerate and process your feelings, especially ones like anger, no matter how strange it might seem to someone else.

9 Managing flashbacks, nightmares, panic attacks and dissociation

Flashbacks, nightmares and panic attacks can be extremely distressing as they seem to have a will of their own and can strike at any time without warning which intensifies your sense of being out of control. The fear of flashbacks, nightmares and panic attacks can have a paralysing effect given that they can overwhelm you at any time making it hard to leave the house or fall asleep. In order to manage flashbacks, nightmares, panic attacks and dissociation, you need to gain control over them. To help you in this you can use some of the skills practiced earlier in the book such as regulating your breathing, monitoring your internal and external reality, and use those grounding techniques that work best for you.

Flashbacks

If you are plagued by flashbacks it is essential that you recognise what they are. First and foremost, flashbacks are precisely that, flash 'backs' to the past. They are incredibly vivid and intense sensory memories of past experiences that have not been processed. They do not represent what is actually happening in the present. In essence they are signals that certain memories of the trauma have not been processed or integrated into your memory system.

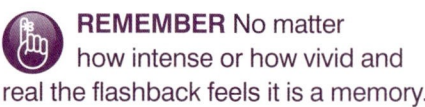 **REMEMBER** No matter how intense or how vivid and real the flashback feels it is a memory.

Managing flashbacks

To manage flashbacks you need to remember that you can feel terrified while not being in any actual danger, and flashbacks are powerful and intense internal experiences that do not reflect external reality (see **Understanding your reactions to CSA and trauma** on page 30). While the external environment may have triggered the flashback such as a smell, sound or visual stimuli reminiscent of past experience, this does not mean that you are in danger. To truly assess the actual danger, you need to monitor not just subjective internal sensations but also objective external reality. During flashbacks, you become over focused on internal cues rather than actual reality. As your alarm system is already on a high alert default setting it fails to register whether the environment is hostile or safe.

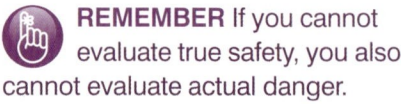 **REMEMBER** If you cannot evaluate true safety, you also cannot evaluate actual danger.

In order to gain control over flashbacks you will need to develop a plan of how to manage them. This can be done prior to an actual flashback, when you are calm and relaxed, which you can then rehearse and practise on a daily basis, so that it becomes automatic.

EXERCISE In your journal try to identify any triggers that have activated flashbacks in the past. Next write down the various ways that you can remind yourself that this is a flashback and keep you grounded in the present. It may be helpful to write down a mantra such as *'This is a memory not a repeat of the trauma. I am remembering, it is not happening now. I am no longer in danger'* or *'This is a flashback and this is a normal reaction to trauma. It happened in the past and the worst is over and it is not happening now.'* Try to keep your statements short to make it easier to remember them. It helps to leave out the details of the trauma as this can intensify the flashback. Practise to find the right words that work for you. When you have found a statement or mantra that suits you, write it down on a sticky note or piece of card. This can then be displayed as a reminder. Alternatively, you can record it on an MP3 player or as a voicemail message on your mobile phone. You can also share these statements with a trusted friend or partner so they can coach you or guide you through it.

Internal dialogue

During flashbacks you may experience an internal dialogue in the present tense describing what is happening such as *'He is coming to get me. She is making me do things I don't like'*. This self-talk, in the present tense, gives the flashback more power and makes it seem more real. The more it feels as though it is happening in the present, the more the alarm system will remain on high alert and set off the appropriate physiological responses. To reduce the power of the flashback you will need to change the tense of the self-talk from the present to the past, such as *'I was attacked. I had to do things I didn't like.'* This places the flashback firmly into the past.

Another technique to manage flashbacks is to imagine that the images that you see are on a TV screen and that you are holding a remote control, which allows you to turn the sound down, or up, to pause the image, or to turn the TV off so that the images fade away.

 REMEMBER You are not going mad. Flashbacks are normal and are a signal that you are dealing with overwhelming experiences and trying to make sense of them.

Plan to manage flashbacks

Alongside your statements, you need to develop a plan for managing flashbacks that also includes regulating your breathing and some grounding techniques. Here is an example that might be helpful to you.

Suggested plan for managing flashbacks

- Breathe fully, with feet on ground (see **Breathing** on page 66).

- Recite your mantra reminding you that this is a memory.

- Check the date on your mobile phone, calendar or daily newspaper.

- Find your anchor or object from the present and look at it, hold it, feel it, smell it – make sure you have access to your grounding smell.

- Adopt your grounding position, or walk around.

- Shift attention from internal to external senses and name them out loud e.g. *'I see the sun shining, I can smell coffee, I can hear the news, today's date is...'*

- Look around the room and notice the colours, the shapes, the objects, the people and listen to the sounds around you – the traffic, voices or washing machine. Identify each sound and say them out loud.

- Evaluate actual external danger by reminding yourself that this is a memory and not actually happening, and that there is no danger.

- Stamp your feet, or grind them on the floor to remind yourself where you are.

- Consciously feel the boundary of your body and skin, the clothes you are wearing, the chair in which you are sitting, the floor supporting you.

- Have an elastic band to hand (or on your wrist), ping it and feel it on your skin. This will remind you of the present and that what you are experiencing internally is in the past.

- If you have lost all sense of where you end and the rest of the world begins, rub your body so you can feel its edges, or wrap yourself in a blanket or scarf and consciously feel it as it surrounds you.

- If you feel very unsafe call a trusted friend who knows the plan.

Feel free to edit and experiment with the plan to find what suits you best. Get support if you need it by letting a trusted, designated friend know about the flashbacks and ask them for help. They can do this by talking to you, holding you or helping you to reconnect with the present while reminding you that you are safe and cared for.

What to do after a flashback

As flashbacks are powerful experiences which drain your energy, it is really important to take care of yourself once the flashback is over. Take a warm relaxing bath or a sleep, have a warm drink or play some soothing music. Take some quiet time for yourself, or look at the items in your mood basket and generally nurture yourself. When you feel ready, write down all you remember about the flashback and how you got through it. This will help you to remember the experience, the triggers, the internal dialogue and how you got through it. It is crucial for your healing to record how you got through the flashback and knowing that will help you get through future ones.

Gaining control over flashbacks

To gain control over flashbacks you will need to explore their content to identify specific aspects of the unprocessed memories (see **Managing and processing memories** on page 83). Try to keep a record of your flashbacks by logging the time and date, any internal or external triggers and the duration and content of the flashback. To help you monitor your progress in managing the flashback and its intensity, it helps if you rank your physical and emotional reactions to the flashback on a scale of one to seven, with one being mildly distressing and seven being highly distressing. The more you monitor your flashbacks the more you will gain control of them and identify the traumatic memories and experiences that need to be processed.

Nightmares

Like flashbacks, nightmares and recurring dreams are reminders of past experiences that need to be processed consciously so that they can be stored as memories. Remember, in essence nightmares are flashbacks that occur while you are asleep. As such they have the same intensity and biochemical responses such as increased heart rate, sweating and palpitations as the actual experience in the past. In many ways, nightmares are more terrifying because the strategies that would help you to control them when you are awake are 'offline'. In addition, the fear of nightmares can make it difficult to go to bed, or fall asleep, leading to insomnia. Even if you are able to fall asleep, the constant waking up from the nightmare makes for very fitful, unsatisfying sleep leaving you feeling exhausted.

REMEMBER Nightmares are the night-time equivalent of flashbacks and are the brain's way of processing experiences and filing them into your memory system. They are not dangerous.

The impact of nightmares

Lack of sleep is not only exhausting but also leaves you feeling tired, irritable and lacking in energy. Fear of going to sleep means that there is no opportunity to recuperate or process new experiences. This can lead to poor concentration, confusion and a sense of not being able to manage even the simplest of tasks. To restore sleep and control over your dreams and nightmares you will need to combine the management of your nightmares with improved sleeping patterns.

WARNING Sleep exhaustion can tempt you to use sleeping tablets. This can help in the short term but they are highly addictive and can lead to dependency.

To restore sleep you may be tempted to take sleeping tablets but be warned that these can lead to dependency. More importantly, they are merely aids to help you sleep which do not process the experience contained in the dreams. If you have no alternative but to use prescribed sleeping tablets, then make sure you use these as a short term measure to relieve exhaustion. It is much better long term if you can develop strategies to aid sleep and manage unpleasant dreams.

Improving sleep patterns

To improve sleep you will need to change your sleep schedule to regulate your sleep pattern. Try to have a set, regular time that you go bed, along with a calming bedtime ritual. Keeping sensory stimuli in the bedroom to an absolute minimum aids sleep so try to avoid using a radio, TV or MP3 player while in bed. It is critical that you make the bedroom into a safe place, or sanctuary, especially if the abuse took place in a bedroom. You can do this by making sure that the sensory cues are different from those of the room in which the abuse took place. This could include the colour scheme, lighting, smell and type of bed clothing. It is also useful to have a comforter, such as a special blanket or a stuffed toy, from the present that can be used in moments of distress to soothe you and remind you that you are in the present not the past.

Sleep can also be more restful if you eat regularly and at least three hours before going to bed as this aids digestion. It helps to be aware which foods give you heartburn or indigestion and which affect your sleep and dreams. Heavy meals, spicy food, too much caffeine or alcohol can all interrupt sleep, as can smoking. Try not to exercise before bed as your body needs to wind down rather than remaining on high alert. To help you relax take a soothing bath with scented candles, wrap yourself in warm towel or bathrobe, and rub your favourite scented moisturiser or body oil onto your skin. A soothing drink such as herbal tea can also help you and your body to wind down.

✓ **ACTIVITY** Find a notebook that you can use as a dream journal and keep this by your bedside with a pen. Whenever you wake as a result of a dream or nightmare, or when you wake up in the morning, record your dream(s) in your journal. Try to include as much information and detailed content as you can, as well as how you felt. This will help you to keep track of your dreams, and identify recurring themes, with which to process and make sense of them.

Record your nightmares and dreams

Remember to record your nightmare, no matter how terrifying, before you try to go back to sleep. Falling asleep after a nightmare in the hope that the nightmare will not return is often futile. Remember if it has not been processed it is much more likely to recur. In recording your dreams you will be able to process their content consciously, and link them to the trauma experiences. This will make it easier to integrate them into your memory system, which in turn will reduce the nightmares.

Processing nightmares

During the daytime when you feel safe and are in a calm state you can read through your nightmares or dreams and consciously reflect on them. This will help you to consider hidden or symbolic messages and what they mean. When you reach the terrifying or upsetting parts, write *'Stop. This is just a dream.'* Practise saying this as it will help you to say the same thing while you are asleep and stop the nightmare.

Alternatively you can discuss your nightmare with a trusted friend or upon re-reading it imagine it as a fictional story. This will allow you to try out two or three different positive endings, allowing you to re-write the outcome of the nightmare.

These more positive endings can then be rehearsed and inserted into your dream or nightmare while you are asleep. It is useful to rehearse your re-written endings before going to sleep so that you can insert the alternative ending more easily.

Lucid dreaming

To further reduce the power nightmares have over you, you can practise **lucid dreaming**. This means knowing that you are dreaming while still dreaming. This can be achieved by regularly recalling dreams, rehearsing alternative endings and practising auto or self-suggestion to remind yourself that you are dreaming. With practise you will become more aware that you are dreaming and will be able to control how the dream develops and control its ending. All these strategies will help you to process the content of your nightmares and dreams and reduce their power over you to allow for more restful and satisfying sleep.

Remember sleep has powerful restorative effects and can aid your recovery by integrating memories as well as inspiring insight and improving problem solving skills.

Panic attacks

Like flashbacks and nightmares, panic attacks are so overwhelming that they can appear life threatening making it hard to manage them. One way to help you manage panic attacks is to understand the link they have to unprocessed feelings and experiences. It is also useful to identify any anxieties or areas of stress in your life that trigger the panic attacks. In doing this you can find alternative, more healthy ways of expressing your anxieties and feelings.

Mimicking sensations

A good way of learning to manage panic attacks is to mimic the sensations of the panic attack in a safe setting. This will show you that the sensations in panic attacks are not life threatening and can be controlled. For instance try breathing through a straw to simulate panicky breathing, tense your muscles to resemble muscle tension or spin in a chair to mimic the dizziness and disorientation that accompanies panic attacks. In mimicking these sensations in a safe setting and learning how to manage them you can then transfer and use these skills in an actual panic attack.

Plan for panic attacks

As you mimic the sensations of a panic attack try to identify what helps to ground you and restore control. List all the things that help you and make sure that you include them in your plan for managing panic attacks. Below is a suggested plan that you can adapt or edit to include what is most helpful to you.

REMEMBER This is a panic attack. You are not going to die. The panic attack is harmless, it will pass and you will be fine.

Suggested plan for panic attacks

- Stop, take a break and try to think about what it is that is making you panic.

- Check and regulate your breathing (see **Breathing** on page 66) by breathing fully and consciously.

- If you are hyperventilating, hold each breath for three counts. If necessary use paper bag technique (see **Breathing** on page 66).

- Touch your anchor.

- Sit down somewhere comfortable.

- Try to think positive thoughts.

- Remind yourself that you are not going to die, that the attack is harmless and will soon pass and that you will be fine.

- Rather than run away from the scene, tell yourself that you will stay for one or two minutes. When that time is up try to stay for another couple of minutes. If this proves too much then leave.

Dissociation

Dissociation is an adaptive part of your emotional immune system to protect you from traumatic experiences. When traumatic experiences, or memories of them, threaten to overpower you, dissociating or 'tuning out' is a way to avoid being overwhelmed. To aid survival, dissociation also anaesthetises the intensity of both physical and emotional pain. While not all survivors of CSA dissociate, many do and yet are not always aware that they do. To check whether you dissociate and how it impacts on you, look at the exercise below.

EXERCISE In your journal ask yourself the following questions. Do you find yourself detaching? How frequently and when does this happen? Does dissociating concern you or cause you problems? Are you extra sensitive to certain topics or abuse related cues? What particularly upsets you? What are the triggers? You might also consider keeping a diary of dissociation, like the one for flashbacks, to record the frequency, triggers for and the duration of dissociation.

Grounding strategies

As in flashbacks it is vital that you ground yourself, using as many sensory cues as you can as soon as you are aware of dissociating. Try to reconnect to your body and the physical world by briskly rubbing your arms or legs, or by planting your feet on the ground. Alternatively touch or hold something cold such as an ice cold aluminium can or drink, or a packet of frozen peas. You could also put your hand in a bucket of ice or have a cold shower. Having a hot drink can also help, as long as you are careful not to burn yourself.

Eating or drinking something with a strong taste or texture, such as chilli or lemon, will also help to ground you and to feel bodily sensation. Alternatively eat something you enjoy such as a crunchy apple or something cold such as ice cream or sucking an ice cube. Notice how it feels as you chew it, or as it melts in your mouth and travels down your throat to your stomach. Be mindful of avoiding strong coffee or tea as this might increase arousal.

Remember to use your grounding smell, or smell something strong such as lemon zest or a strong spice. Make sure though that the smell you choose does not remind you of the past, or is linked to your traumatic experiences. Put on some energising or uplifting music to make you more alert, as long as it does not remind you of the past. To reduce disconnection from your body, you could dance or do some light exercises such as sit ups. Alternatively go for a walk or run outside to reorient you in your physical surroundings. Be careful if you have prolonged episodes of dissociation, as going outside may not be safe as you could get lost.

TOP TIP Record your voice on your mobile phone or MP3 player, or send a voice message to yourself noting the date, your age, where you currently live and the names of family members, partner, children or pets.

As in flashbacks, look around the room and name each object as you see it. Hearing your voice out loud will help you to remain connected to the present and increase your awareness of your surroundings. You can also record your voice on your mobile phone or MP3 player, or send a voice message to yourself noting the date, your age, where you currently live and the names of family members, partner, children or pets. This will help you to remember that you are not in the traumatic situation from the past, and that you are safe.

Alternatively, you could read aloud to yourself, look at and describe your favourite painting or poster, or sing a song from the present day as loud as you possibly can. If possible speak to someone who knows what you are experiencing and can help by talking to you. They can also remind you of the present time and your location by holding your hand, and maintaining eye contact so that you can reconnect to your body.

If you are sitting down, get up and walk into another room, especially if you are feeling paralysed or are out of contact with your external surroundings. Stepping outside for a minute can also help. If safe, go out for a walk, go to a café, or go shopping where there are other people around. As you do this try to make a point of noticing the ordinary things around you to remind yourself that your environment is not threatening to you. If the room you are in when you dissociate is dimly lit, walk around and turn on all the lights. This is especially good if you get frightened at night.

When you have reconnected to yourself and the physical world, write down all you can remember about the dissociative episode, including the trigger. Try to record where you went in your head, what you saw and what helped to ground you. Keeping a record in your journal will help you to monitor the triggers, frequency and duration of dissociative episodes. This can help you to identify what is making you dissociate and how to manage and control these episodes. Ultimately it can help you to reduce their frequency so that you remain more grounded in the present.

⚠️ **WARNING Be safe, do not drive, iron or operate machinery if you suffer frequent bouts of dissociation. Make sure any young children, pets or dependents are safe.**

10 Managing memories

Many survivors of childhood sexual abuse have unclear or fragmented memories of the abuse. Sometimes these are fleeting images, sounds or smells which lack context, sequential narrative or are detached from any meaning. The degree of memory recall will vary from person to person. Thus you could have only partial memories, no memories at all or full recall.

The overwhelming nature of CSA can make it hard to process the experience and integrate it into the memory system. If it is accompanied by dissociation or avoidance it may be even harder to store the experience. As a result the memories are stored and remain 'on line' at the same intensity as when first experienced. This can result in flashbacks, intrusive memories or nightmares.

 REMEMBER Experiences and memories that are suppressed are twice as likely to resurface.

How much do you need to remember?

There is considerable debate about to what extent it is necessary to recall all memories. Focusing on full memory recall can create more pressure on you. It is important that you have a choice as to what extent you want to recover memories. The dynamic nature of memory will limit full recall of every experience and event. Only you can decide how much detail you wish to remember. Do not be pressurised either by yourself, others or professionals.

Only you can decide when you have enough memories to validate your experiences and work on processing them. Avoid searching for something that may not be possible to recover. Delving into past memories is only worthwhile if there is something to be gained, and must be paced to suit your stage of recovery. If you have quite clear memories, although distressing ones, then it may not be the best use of your resources to continue to probe. Over processing does not necessarily generate any real benefits.

If your memories are fragmented or sketchy and you want to improve recall then it makes sense to do some memory work to flesh these out. If however retrieving memories always destabilises you, you may be better to leave memory work until later in your recovery.

If you suffer from intrusive memories, flashbacks or nightmares, which consistently make you feel worse, then it will help to process these. However, you will need to ensure you have mastered some of the grounding techniques and are more able to regulate your reactions.

If you have no memories at all but sense that something may have happened, do not focus exclusively on searching for abuse memories. Doing so could lead to fabrication and leave you vulnerable to false memories. Try to stay in the present and allow memories to emerge gradually rather than delving as this can have severe consequences. Do not be persuaded by others, including professionals that you must probe and find evidence through memories as this can be fraught with problems.

WARNING Work with what you have rather than delve and risk false memories.

Memory recall

To help you decide you need to reflect on your goals for recalling memories. The exercise below can help you in this.

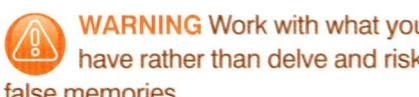**EXERCISE** Take some time to reflect on your goals for recalling memories. Are you plagued by intrusive memories, flashbacks and nightmares? Do you want to improve the quality of your life? Do you need confirmation of your abuse? If so then processing and integrating memories may be invaluable as long as you do it at a pace that suits you.

The danger of over-processing memories

If you already have clear memories and are not haunted by unprocessed memories, then it may not be necessary. Over-processing memories can lead to elaborated, distorted and inaccurate memories which can result in further difficulties. If you are searching for memories to gain clarity or make sense of your experiences then memory work will be beneficial. Avoid focusing on 100% recall as this may not be possible to achieve.

Memories are not the only source of validation

If you want to recall memories to confirm your experience then you may need to set a limit on how much is necessary to remember rather than keep searching. Memory recall is not always the best, or only, source of validation of CSA. You may need to seek out additional sources, such as others who have been abused by the same person. This is often the case in clerical abuse. Remember that you need to trust yourself rather than trying to search for evidence to convince others.

REMEMBER The dynamic nature of memory means that you may not be able to restore full memory so you need to set a gauge that is 'good enough' for you that validates your experiences.

Pressure to recall memories

Pressure to recall memories can risk a sense of failure and promote self-suggestion. In addition, pressure from others can lead to potential false memories. To prevent this it is critical that you do not try to recall too hard and take the pressure off. Allow memories to emerge when you are ready to manage them.

Most importantly, remember that memory is subjective and dynamic and that we do not store or recall memories like a video recording. Commonly memory provides a general sense of what happened. This means they are often imperfect and contain gaps in the details which we naturally try to fill to create a narrative.

The reliability of memory

The reliability of memory is largely accurate but can be distorted or elaborated due to our attempts to gain meaning and fill in gaps. This is more likely if the memories are fuzzy or there are large pieces that are missing. It is also more likely if you have been taught to doubt your memory through denial or minimisation of the CSA.

Denial and minimisation

Denial and minimisation can lead to having no recollection of CSA at all, which is technically false memory if abuse has occurred. Equally rehearsing, imagining, self-suggestion or suggestion by others can also lead to distortions and strengthen the imagined memory and risk of false memories.

Lack of detail

Lack of detail does not invalidate the memory. It is much better to work with the content of what is recalled, even if these are embedded in intrusive memories, flashbacks or nightmares. Remember these all represent unprocessed memories which signal parts of your experiences that need attention to be processed and integrated into your memory system.

The content of flashbacks and nightmares contain fragmented, partial or elaborated memories of your experiences which trigger the same physiological responses as when the trauma occurred. This is why they are so vivid and feel like you are re-experiencing the trauma. In avoiding them they remain more 'alive' demanding even more attention.

Managing and processing memories

To manage and process memories you need to identify the content of any recollections and keep a record of these. This will be difficult if they are intrusive and overwhelming, and you may need to leave in depth memory work until some way into your recovery. It is more effective to do this when you have mastered grounding skills and are more able to regulate your reactions.

It is also more helpful to try to process memories when you are calm and relaxed rather than overwrought. Integration of memories is a process that persists throughout the recovery journey and is best when you feel more in control of your trauma reactions.

Eye movement desensitisation and reprocessing (EMDR)

One effective way of processing traumatic memories is through **eye movement desensitisation and reprocessing** (EMDR).This can only be done with a practitioner who has been specially trained in this technique. This method helps to process the traumatic experiences through rapid eye movement and can reduce the intensity of feelings attached to the traumatic memory. While EMDR can be hugely beneficial, some survivors may wish to process memories using more conventional techniques. Remember it is important that you choose what is best for you.

Cues to aid memory recall

If you have no memories of CSA you could try to recall other aspects of your life at that time. This can be done by trying to remember a typical day in which you try to recall a day in your life around that time. You might think about who woke you up, got you dressed and took you to school. Make a list of your friends and teachers at school, and your favourite lessons. Who picked you up from school, gave you tea and got you ready for bed. Such everyday memories can help you to recall other associated memories.

Photographs of you before, during and after the abuse can also aid memory recall. You could put these into an album alongside photographs of family members, friends and the abuser(s) if you have any. Such visual cues can be quite powerful in helping you to recall memories and feelings that you felt at that time.

83

Drawing your childhood home can also aid memory recall. You could draw the house or flat in which you lived at the time of the abuse, including floor plans of the rooms and the layout of the room in which you were most often abused. Include as many things as you can remember such as how the furniture was arranged, where windows and doors were, the colour scheme as well as any associated smells or feelings.

Visiting the home and neighbourhood in which you lived when you were abused can also be powerful aids to memory recall. As this can be potentially distressing it is helpful if you have someone you trust with you should you feel overwhelmed.

In combination these can all aid memory recall but they may need to be explored over time. Be mindful that the memories may not return in a rush but emerge gradually when you are ready to tolerate them. They might also recur through your dreams or as flashbacks. You need to view these as signals that a memory is returning that needs to be processed.

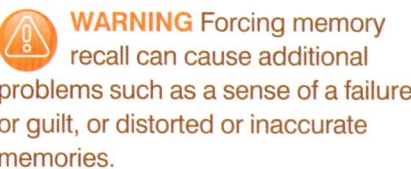 **WARNING** Forcing memory recall can cause additional problems such as a sense of a failure or guilt, or distorted or inaccurate memories.

Assessment

Assessing whether, and to what extent, you wish to restore memory will mean exploring whether you want to have full detailed memories. Are you happy to have general memories that are 'good enough', do you need full recall or do you prefer not to delve into memories at all? Alternatively you might wish to put any memory work on hold for the moment and reassess at a later point when stability has improved.

 EXERCISE To assess whether memory work is for you, make a list of the advantages and disadvantages. Your list of advantages might include the desire to improve the quality of your life by reducing intrusive memories, flashbacks or nightmares; to feel more in control; to undo the freeze response and release trapped energy; to clarify what happened; to give meaning to your experiences; to legitimise what happened; to change the way you think about yourself; to reduce self-blame; to understand the impact of CSA and trauma; or to restore reality and perception. Your list of disadvantages might include decrease in your quality of life; destabilisation if you cannot remember; sense of failure or shame; or feeling paralysed or trapped by your need to remember. Do add any other advantages and disadvantages you can think of. Reflect on these to help you decide.

Pacing memory work

Before starting memory work you need to assess your level of functioning to ensure that you will be able to regulate your feelings. It helps to review your list of triggers of flashbacks and to make one for intrusive memories. It is also wise to avoid some of the most distressing triggers until you feel more in control of your reactions. Effective memory processing should proceed at a manageable pace for you so you feel in control. It is best to work towards memory processing gradually when you are calm and stable, and to reflect on your progress. If the memory work is too fast, or conducted during crisis points, it will become overwhelming and can increase post traumatic reactions.

Whenever you focus on recalling a memory make sure you have a block of uninterrupted time to really engage in the process. Make sure that you do not rush this and allow time to do this over several days. Also remember to you treat yourself to a reward afterwards.

Recording your memories

As memories return write down the general points rather than the details of the memory. If writing is difficult, find another way to record it such as painting or drawing, making a collage or sculpture, writing a song or poem that encapsulates the memory, or make an audio recording. Once the initial impression has been recorded, revisit the memory to include more details including as many sensory cues as possible.

Try to recall what you saw, sensed, smelt, heard, touched or tasted during the experience and your body position. Include the sequence of events, what happened, what were you doing and thinking, what were your reactions, your feelings and your physical sensations. Reflect on what the experience meant to you, what was the worst bit, how did it impact on you then and your life since, and how it has changed you. Allow yourself to experience feelings and sensations without judgement. Consider the hardest part of the experience to get used to. What are you not able to do anymore and where you are stuck?

Processing memories

As you revisit the memory, more details will emerge which can be added into your account. Remember every time you read, look at or listen to it and make amendments you are processing the memory and integrating it. This will help you gain meaning and reduce flashbacks, nightmares and intrusive memories.

When you are happy with your account discuss the memory with someone you trust, and make any changes. Once you have an account that you are satisfied with revisit it with self-compassion and empathy to allow the full range of your emotions to emerge without judgment. You may wish to put your account somewhere safe to look at whenever you need to.

WARNING Don't force the memory and stop if you feel overwhelmed. Ground yourself and revisit the memory at a later point.

Tolerating uncertainty

If despite such focused memory work no memories of CSA are recalled, or they remain fragmented or patchy, then you will need to work on tolerating uncertainty. Try to rely on what you do know. Use your body as a resource and store of memory, rather than pursuing the quest for perfect memory recall.

Hypnosis

You may feel tempted to undergo hypnosis to help memory recall. While this can be helpful, there is no guarantee that recalling memories under hypnosis will be any more accurate than if recalled without hypnosis. If you do want to try hypnosis make sure you find a reputable practitioner who also has therapeutic experience and who can provide emotional support as memories return.

REMEMBER Only you can choose to what extent you wish to engage in memory processing. Do not be influenced by others, including professionals.

Drugs that block memories

There has been considerable research into developing drugs that can block memories at a biochemical level, which can be administered either pre- or post-trauma. While drugs designed to eradicate traumatic memories sound highly desirable it is vital that you recognise that currently their effects are only partial. They may not work for each individual.

More importantly they may have a negative effect as blocking memories which signal that something is wrong will prevent emotional processing. These drugs will merely block the memory without helping you to process your abuse experience. As such they may be most helpful in the short term to block intrusive memories until emotional regulation is mastered.

REMEMBER drugs that block memories will not integrate your experiences which could result in lack of continuity and confusion. Ultimately this could interfere with the recovery process and the potential for post traumatic growth in which you can truly triumph over trauma.

11 Managing negative thoughts and negative beliefs

We are all vulnerable to negative thoughts and beliefs but these can be inflamed by trauma and heightened anxiety. Being in survival mode can also result in more biased thinking. This will make you more vulnerable to misjudgements that tend to reinforce fears or anxieties and prolong pain and misery.

As biased thinking is often deeply embedded, it is critical to identify and challenge them to find alternative ways of thinking and reduce being controlled by them. You also need to understand the impact they have on you, and replace them with more objective beliefs. This will enable you to improve your self-esteem, your mood and your view of the future.

Negative beliefs

Negative beliefs and distorted thinking usually consist of negative thoughts about the self, others, the world and the future. Sometimes these are so habitual that they become automatic and seem to occur outside awareness. Some negative beliefs are distorted perceptions inserted by the abuser(s) which you could not challenge as a child and therefore included them into your belief system.

Negative self-beliefs

Negative self-beliefs such as *'I am to blame'*, *'I am bad'* or *'I am worthless'* infect your developing self-identity. This ultimately leads you to filter the world through the abusers eyes, voice and actions. As these become incorporated into your sense of self, you may not even be aware of your negative thoughts or how they impact on you.

Negative self-beliefs are reflected in your inner critical voice which constantly undermines you and acts as a saboteur stripping you of self-esteem. They also lead to the false belief that you were to blame for the abuse and thus deserve all the bad things that happen to you.

Negative beliefs about others

Negative beliefs about others centre around other people being untrustworthy, rejecting, or potentially abusive. Your negative beliefs about the world focus on the belief that it is hostile and full of danger and disappointment. Such beliefs emphasise your lack of safety and trust which leads to defensive reactions such as disconnection from self and from others and the world. Negative beliefs about the future revolve around beliefs that you will be haunted by the CSA forever.

Feelings as facts

Distorted beliefs are also seen in the belief that feelings are facts and the more you feel something the more real it must be. For example, because you FEEL flawed, you FEEL everyone else will think so too. This can lead you to believe that you will never be able to have a healthy relationship. Left unchallenged, negative beliefs can lead to pervasive anguish, despondency and thoughts of suicide.

REMEMBER Negative beliefs about yourself may have been inserted by the abuser(s) and do not reflect reality.

Challenging negative beliefs

To reduce the impact of negative thoughts and beliefs you need to recognise them along with any misinterpretations and misjudgements associated with them. Once recognised it will be possible to challenge them by asking key questions such as to what extent is my thinking biased? Is there anything to support these biases? What is the evidence against such biases?

While this can be hard at first it is worth persevering. Once you have evaluated your negative beliefs, you can begin finding alternative thoughts that are more objective and not coloured by distorted perceptions. To explore any fears changing beliefs you need to consider what is the worst that can happen in adopting new thoughts, and how you would manage these?

With focused practice you will find it increasingly easier to create more balanced and objective re-statements enabling you to change biased thinking and beliefs to have a more authentic view of yourself. This will permit more realistic and positive self-appraisals which will reduce distress, regulate your mood and facilitate healing.

Common biases in thinking

There are a number of common biases in thinking that support negative beliefs and it is worth considering each of these in turn.

All or nothing thinking is the tendency to only see extremes rather than the full range of possibilities. For instance you are either good or un-redeemably bad, brilliant or a complete failure. All or nothing thinking is usually directed at self-appraisals but can also be applied to others who you see as either totally trustworthy or totally untrustworthy, or situations which are either a complete success or utter failure.

Such thinking is self-limiting and increases anxiety and disappointment. Challenging such thinking can allow for a range of possible interpretations, reduce perfectionism and allow for opportunities for change.

Over-generalisation is when you draw conclusions based on isolated events and apply these to a wide range of situations. A common example of this is seeing one negative event as an indication of everything being negative and assuming that outcomes will always be negative. This is particularly seen in the false belief that because you were abused by a man all men are abusers and not to be trusted. This can undermine your trust in men and prevent you from having a healthy relationship with a man.

Another form of over-generalisation is **mislabelling** which is the tendency to create a totally negative image on the basis of one single, minor deficiency. Thus one minor flaw or attribute is used to totally negate the whole person or self. Linked to this is **catastrophisation** which is the tendency to predict and expect the very worst in any one situation based on one minor difficulty. While this is primarily used to prepare for the worst possible scenario to avoid disappointment, it leads to increased and unwarranted anxiety and worry.

Another common thinking bias is **mental filtering** in which positive aspects of a situation are filtered out leaving no choice but to dwell exclusively on negative aspects. Filtering out all positive experiences, thoughts and feelings keep you locked into a spiral of negativity from which there seems to be no escape. This can lead to a very negative view of change and a better future.

Alongside mental filtering is **disqualifying the positive** in which a positive aspect of self, others or a situation, is downgraded, rejected or dismissed as unimportant. This is often seen when you transform positive experiences or feelings into something negative, leading to distorted beliefs despite contradictory evidence.

Another aspect of mental filtering is **magnification** and **minimisation** in which negative events are exaggerated in importance and positive events are underestimated. In magnification you might exaggerate mistakes and deficiencies totally out of proportion to reality. With minimisation you play down positive attributes leading to negative self-image as the positive is always cancelled out.

Minimisation is also seen when survivors try to reduce the impact and effects of CSA by maintaining that the abuse was not that bad and had no negative effect. Such denial serves an important function in enabling you to manage the CSA experiences without having to work through them.

Jumping to conclusions is another common example of distorted thinking in which negative conclusions are drawn which are not justified by the facts. A common example is *'Because I feel ashamed and blame myself for the abuse, everyone will also blame me.'* Two commonly associated aspects of jumping to conclusions is **mind reading** and **fortune telling**.

While mind reading is in part a protective mechanism developed in childhood to predict the abusers thoughts, feelings or behaviour, it is not always accurate. It tends to always assume negative reactions due to your heightened alarm setting. In addition, when you mind read you come out of your own frame of reference and enter the other persons. This further reduces the opportunity to monitor the full range of feelings or thoughts.

Fortune telling is a form of mind reading in which you believe that you can predict all future outcomes. This is rarely based on objective evidence but is primarily driven by fear and projection. It is a form of 'psyching' oneself up for the worst case scenario so as not to be disappointed or to be prepared for the worst possible threat. This is an understandable defence mechanism which aims to predict and thereby control behaviour and outcome.

Due to the intensity of your emotions you can be driven by **emotional reasoning** in which you assume that feelings are facts, and an accurate reflection of reality and truth. This is based on a common assumption that the more intensely or vividly something is felt the more real it is. In the same way that thinking can be distorted, so can feelings especially when your alarm system is constantly on high alert. Common examples of this are assuming that if you feel bad you must be bad, or because you FEEL guilty you must BE guilty.

REMEMBER Feelings are signals from the body and not necessarily facts.

Emotional reasoning can lead to **personalisation** in which you assume responsibility when there is none. A classic example is assuming that because you experienced an erection or an orgasm during the sexual abuse you must have wanted it. It is also seen in taking things very personally in assuming that bad or unpleasant experiences are specifically directed at you and must be your fault. Thus, if a situation doesn't go well it must be because of something you did or didn't do and you deserve to be punished.

Seeing yourself as the cause of bad events, and the belief that you deserve punishment further fuels self-blame and self-criticism. You take responsibility for things that really are not your fault. Self-criticism is fuelled by a harsh **internal self-critic** who labels you as *'useless'* or *'stupid'* or calls you names. Such name calling may reflect criticism and negative beliefs inserted by the abuser(s) which sabotaged the development of a more positive self-image. In combination, these all serve to maintain an already poor self-image.

To compensate for any perceived flaws you may impose unrealistic expectations on yourself and become **perfectionist** in your thinking and behaviour. This is reflected in 'should' statements of how you should or ought to be or behave. As these expectations and criteria are unrealistic and virtually impossible to achieve your strivings are destined to failure. This in turn leads to a sense of failure, and even more guilt and self-criticism. This fuels low self-esteem rather than focusing on realistic and achievable ways of creating change.

Many survivors also have **high expectations** of others that are impossible to achieve leading to a repetitive cycle of being disappointed in them. This confirms the belief that others will always let you down and cannot be trusted, leading to disconnection from others and further isolation and loneliness.

As can be seen negative thoughts and beliefs can have a huge impact on self-esteem and create obstacles to recovery and healing. To help you identify your negative thoughts and beliefs try the following exercise to reappraise your thoughts and find more accurate alternatives.

EXERCISE Read through the range of negative thoughts and beliefs presented above and highlight which ones apply to you. List these in your journal along with an example of each negative thought or belief. Next try to identify any biases in your thinking and beliefs and how these shape your thinking and behaviour. Once you have identified biased thinking you can begin to challenge this by asking yourself *'Is there any evidence to support this thought or belief?'* and *'What is the evidence that does not support this thought or belief?'* As you write down the evidence for and against negative thoughts or beliefs you can begin to consider alternative ways of thinking.

Next, write down any alternative thoughts or beliefs which more accurately reflect reality. Before putting these into practice and testing them out it helps to consider *'What is the worst that can happen if I adopt this alternative thought or belief?'* and *'How would I cope if the worst happened?'* By exploring your fears around changing negative thinking you will be able to anticipate obstacles and prepare for the management of alternative thoughts. Take time to do this for each negative thought and belief and remember to pace yourself when testing out alternative thoughts.

Reappraising your thoughts

Over time you will find that you are able to reappraise old patterns of thinking and beliefs, as well as new situations and experiences. You will also be able to check your thoughts for any biases more easily. This will help you to navigate your world with more realistic appraisals and not be restricted by negative biases that serve to undermine your self-esteem and self-worth.

To support the reappraisal of biased thinking and beliefs you need to develop greater self-compassion and self-forgiveness. To facilitate this try to see what happened to you through a child's eyes rather than filtering it through an adult perspective. In developing compassion for yourself you will be able to access empathy for the child. You will recognise that you were not responsible for your abuse and had no choice in your reactions and behaviour.

This will help to minimise self-blame, guilt and shame by recognising that your reactions were normal within the context of being abused. You will be able to forgive yourself and begin to let go of self-criticism and negative self-beliefs and thoughts. It will also allow you to redistribute responsibility for the abuse and reduce the tendency to take responsibility unnecessarily. This will free you up to only take responsibility for what is truly yours.

TOP TIP To develop compassion for yourself try to see the CSA through the child's eyes rather than filtering it through an adult perspective.

Ultimately, identifying and reappraising your negative thoughts and beliefs will enable you take more control and remove obstacles to your recovery. You will begin to reconnect to yourself and others in a more authentic way, reduce distortion of reality and begin to accept yourself.

12 Managing harmful behaviours: self-injury and substance misuse

To manage unrelenting emotional pain, overwhelming thoughts and PTSD symptoms, you may resort to self-harming behaviours. The spectrum of self-harm ranges from passive self-harm, such as not looking after yourself through to active self-injury, including eating disorders and substance misuse. Passive self-harm includes lack of self-care, poor hygiene, self-neglect, lack of boundaries, not being able to say 'no' or express basic needs. It also includes the suppression of pleasurable feelings.

In contrast, active, deliberate self-harm consists of direct self-injury such as cutting, burning, self-mutilation or persistent suicide attempts. Or you might manage your emotional pain, or regulate your mood through alcohol, drugs, food or addictive behaviours such as gambling, shopping or sex.

EXERCISE To identify self-harming behaviours, in your journal make a list of the ways in which you could be harming yourself. Be sure to include passive as well as active self-harm such lack of self-care, inability to express your needs, poor diet, or lack of balance between work, rest and play. Also include any addictive behaviour such as excessive use of alcohol or drugs, gambling, shopping or sex. Include any behaviour that puts you at risk, as well as acts of deliberate self-injury. To keep track of self-harming behaviour you could monitor these by including any triggers to self-injury, how often this occurs and the consequences of self-harm.

Function of self-injury

Self-harm and self-injury can be used in a variety of ways. These range from a way to escape emotions, cope with crises, or to calm and comfort you when you are overwrought. It is also a way to restore control or to justify nurturing yourself through tending to your wounds.

Alternatively, you may use alcohol or drugs to block out intrusive memories, control flashbacks, or to help you sleep or avoid nightmares. Or you may use self-injury as a way to manage tension or anxiety, or to numb you by anaesthetising your pain. Self-injury can also be used to bring you out of a dissociative state, and make you feel more real and alive. You may also use self-injury to confirm your existence, to externalise inner pain, to see blood or as a way to cleanse you from toxic feelings.

Over time self-injury can become compulsive and addictive whereby you no longer have control over such behaviours. Whatever your reason for self-injury it is necessary to identify what function it has in your life.

EXERCISE Identifying the function of self-harm and self-injury in your life is the first step in learning to manage these behaviours. Look at the list you made in the previous exercise and reflect on what purpose self-harm has in your life and how it regulates your feelings and mood.

Cycle of self-injury

You will also need to identify the cycle of self-injury behaviour. You may find that as self-injury is preceded by feelings of being engulfed by mental pain, intense feelings of anger, sadness, or despair, out of control physical sensations or negative self-beliefs. As these threaten to overpower you, panic and terror takes over leading to a compulsion to self-injure. As you cut or hurt yourself, the body's natural opiates, known as **endorphins**, are released which numb the pain and replace it with a sense of calm and relief. This release makes you feel more in control, or more able to cope or function.

Alternatively, you may already be numb through dissociation, and to exit this state of deadness you self-injure in order to experience a sense of aliveness or euphoria. This confirms your existence and allows you to feel more grounded. Once the positive aspects of the self-injury have worn off, feelings of shame, guilt, self-hate and self-disgust begin to emerge, until the need to self-injure recurs.

To help you to stop the cycle of self-injury you will need to identify the triggers that lead to either emotional overload or dissociation.

EXERCISE In your journal make a list of the triggers that lead to either emotional overload or dissociation. These can be either internal or external, and can include trauma associated signals, as well as critical messages from others. Self-injury can also be triggered by a sense of rejection or abandonment. Making a list of your triggers will alert you to the stimuli that make you vulnerable to self-harm. With this awareness you can pre-empt when self-injury might occur and try to find alternative ways of managing emotional overload or dissociation (see **Managing flashbacks, nightmares, panic attacks and dissociation** on page 70).

REMEMBER The need for self-injury is a signal of unexpressed feelings which do not have to be acted upon.

Alternative ways of regulating emotions

In finding alternative ways of regulating your emotional states you will be able to reduce the need to self-injure. These may be difficult to begin with as self-injury is hard to give up because it has been effective and worked well in the past. If you find it difficult to stop the self-injury then it is essential that you minimise the harm to yourself until you are able to stop. If you cut yourself make sure that the implements used to cut are sterilised. To reduce infection, ensure sure that you clean and dress any wounds carefully. Also to avoid further risk of injury make sure you do not drink alcohol or take drugs.

Useful strategies

Useful strategies to reduce self-harm and self-injury include replacing blood with a red marker pen, or replacing the pain of cutting with snapping a rubber band on your wrist or ankle. To bring you out of dissociation try squeezing an ice cube, or holding a cold aluminium can. A cold shower or chewing strongly flavoured food stuff such as chilli, ginger root, raw onion or a lemon also eases numbing. To establish greater control and reduce self-injury you need to find the best way of grounding yourself.

Grounding techniques

To help you it is vital to employ the range of grounding techniques that you have already identified as effective for you (see **Restoring control and grounding techniques** on page 55). Make a list of which ones work best for you and try to adapt them to managing self-harm and self-injury. Remember to use all five senses and try to engage in the full range of your emotions. You can also try to connect with someone you trust by phone, email, text or face to face.

A good way to stay in your present reality is to find something that keeps your hands and brain occupied and which allows you to become totally absorbed in a task. If you are haunted by your by internal critical voice then engage it in a dialogue to challenge negative message and replace them with more compassionate ones.

You can also try the **15 minute technique** in which you delay self-injury by 15 minutes by distracting yourself through doing a crossword puzzle or sudoko, or writing in your journal. Alternatively make lists of your ten favourite films, books, songs, paintings, plays, poems or people. After 15 minutes, try to delay for a further 15 minutes and so on. During such distraction the need to self-injure may subside and you will not need to cut or hurt yourself. In addition it will demonstrate that you can exert some control over your compulsion to self-injure.

Alternative ways of communication

Once you have found ways to manage self-injury you can support these by finding alternative ways of communicating your distress. You could practice more effective communication skills to help you to talk and connect to others. In communicating with others, and sharing your fears and vulnerabilities, you will begin to release unexpressed feelings which will reduce your sense of shame and loneliness. This will lead to more effective emotional processing and thereby reduce the need to self-injure and self-medicate.

Self-medication

If you have become dependent on alcohol or drugs to regulate your emotions you will need to seek specialist support to help you to reduce your dependency. This can be extremely difficult and painful especially as the feelings that have been suppressed through alcohol or drugs will re-emerge. It is vital to link self-medication and suppressed emotions to CSA and trauma so that you can process these in a more healthy way.

Depending on the degree of self-medication you may need to consider whether you need to enter a residential detoxification or rehabilitation programme to help you on your road to recovery. Alternatively, you may find the support and help available through 12-step fellowship programmes such as Alcohol Anonymous (AA) or Narcotics Anonymous (NA) more suitable for you. There are now a number of specialist 12-step fellowship programmes to help with a vast range of addictions including food, gambling and shopping as well as love and sex addiction.

Giving up self-injury

Finally, it helps to recognise that reducing self-harm and self-injury can feel like a loss which needs to be mourned. Self-injury, alcohol, food or drugs will have become a reliable and predictable way of altering mood or avoiding feelings. To give up such behaviours can be terrifying and feel like the loss of a trusted companion or reliable friend.

This can lead to resistance as you fear further loss of control. Before you can tackle giving up self-harm and self-injury you must make sure you have mastered alternative ways of regulating your emotions. Most importantly, remember to pace to yourself to optimise your chances of success in replacing self-injury behaviours with more healthy alternatives.

Suicidal thoughts

Self-injury and self-harm can also be a way of managing suicidal thoughts and suicide attempts. You may use self-injury as a way to ward off suicidal feelings, or as an alternative to suicide. Or you may use self-injury as a form of '**russian roulette**' whereby you risk that self-injury could lead to death. Here the motivation is not necessarily to die but the cessation of pain. If you are preoccupied with thoughts of suicide or actively suicidal, it is vital that you seek professional help.

WARNING If self-injury is out of control or you have persistent thoughts about suicide you will need to put this book aside and seek professional help.

Safety plan

If you are feeling suicidal you will need a safety plan. Your safety plan must include a list of your support network, both personal and professional, as well your doctors contact details and a list of specialist services such as Samaritans. You could draw up a contract with a trusted friend that if suicidal thoughts threaten to overpower you, that you will contact them to discuss these. If you have several trusted friends you might consider a rota system for extra support.

13 Managing shame, guilt and self-blame

Shame is like a virus that infects the soul. It is commonly seen in survivors of CSA, alongside guilt and self-blame. Shame is one of the most complicated emotions to resolve as it affects the very core of you. Many survivors often confuse guilt with shame, and yet there are significant differences. In guilt the person has done something for which they can apologise and make amends. In shame the whole of your being feels wrong so you have to apologise for your very existence. Shame is one of the most difficult emotions to let go as there is no way to discharge the feeling. Unlike sadness where you might cry, or anger where you might vent your frustration, there is no channel for release.

The purpose of shame

One way of resolving shame is to have a deeper understanding of its function and how it has affected you. In the words of Nietzsche *'Everyone needs a sense of shame, no one needs to feel ashamed.'* Shame is necessary for survival as it alerts you to the fact that something is wrong about an experience or behaviour. As such it also acts as a prompt to seek help. Shame also guides behaviour so that you do not hurt others or yourself. This was not the case with your abuser(s), who in not feeling shame was able to abuse you.

Whose shame is it?

A good way of understanding your shame is to recognise that it acts as a reminder that your abuse was wrong, not because of what you did, or did not do, but what the abuser(s) did to you. In abusing you, the shame lies solely with your abuser(s). However, because your abuser(s) felt no shame, you had no choice but take on the shame he or she should have felt.

REMEMBER The shame of CSA is not your shame but the abuser's shame that you have taken on.

Taking on the abuser's shame increases any shame you might have felt during the CSA. You may have felt shame for submitting to the CSA, for not telling someone about it, or for having an erection or becoming aroused during the abuse. Whatever the reason(s) for your shame, it is important to recognise that the shame still lies with the abuser(s) for abusing you. Remember you had no choice or control over your reactions while being abused. In addition, your abuser(s) deliberately ensured that you felt pleasure so that you would feel too ashamed to tell. When this is combined with taking on your abuser's shame, it is not surprising that your sense of shame is increased, making it even more crippling. This is why it is vital to redirect your shame where it belongs – onto the abuser(s) rather than yourself.

EXERCISE To help you separate the shame you feel about yourself and your abuser(s), make two columns in your journal. Column one is for the abuser's shame and column two is for yours. Identify and list any shameful acts in each column. Look at these two lists. You will probably find that your list contains relatively small amounts of shame, most of which will be as a result of acts forced on you. This will show how your shame is tied to the shameless acts of your abuser(s). You may also ask yourself whether there is anyone else who has behaved in a shameless way. Or is there anyone else's shame that you have taken on. This could include other family members, or authorities who had a duty of care to safeguard you such as the police, social services, school or, in the case of clerical abuse, the church. To give this shame back to them, write a letter or a poem to the person(s), without sending it. Or you could express this by drawing or painting, or by talking to a trusted friend.

Talking about your shame

Another powerful way to release shame is to talk to people you trust. Shame is a social emotion which shapes and regulates social behaviour. It is an essential part of social interaction which guides behaviour to make us accepted members of families, tribes, cultures and social groups. When we feel ashamed we feel excluded or isolated from others and feel compelled to withdraw, both physically and psychologically. This goes against our basic human need to be connected to others and make things worse as shame festers in isolation and reinforces it.

A recurring conflict in shame is the need to be visible and the need to be invisible. This paradox of needing to be seen, heard and understood but feeling so ashamed that you withdraw from others is paralysing. The shame is further reinforced by negative, shame-based beliefs such as *'I am a bad or shameful person'* or *'I am a mistake'* or *'I am less than.'*

Shame and self-identity

Shame attacks the very core of your being and threatens to destroy your self-identity through self-loathing. This is seen in feelings of self-hatred, a lack of dignity or honour, feeling like 'damaged goods' or feeling that you are so flawed that others will be repulsed by you. Ultimately you end up feeling as though you have no right to exist. This increases neediness and dependency on others to value you and support your self-esteem, which further reinforces a sense of shame.

Shame and the body

Shame also affects how you feel about your body. You may feel that your body has betrayed you, or you see it as an object of scorn, which results in a feeling of revulsion and dislike of your the body. This can lead to believing that your body is defective, or **body dysmorphic disorder**. To manage this **body shame** you might go to great lengths to cover up by hiding your body in shapeless clothing. Or you might exercise excessively to resculpt your body, or seek perfection through extreme cosmetic surgery. Male survivors may body build and use steroids to get the perfect physique or to look stronger. Alternatively, you might punish yourself with deliberate disfigurement, starving yourself, or gaining vast quantities of weight to hide behind. Or your shame can lead you to deny your body any bodily pleasures, leading to **sexual shame**, making it hard to enter into intimate relationships. A further cover up might be to display your body in sexually provocative ways to 'prove' that your body is attractive.

Social shame

Shame is also seen in extreme self-consciousness in ordinary social situations. For example, eating or drinking in the presence of others can become difficult. You may also fear drawing attention to yourself in public which can lead to social phobia which further distances you from others. Your default setting is that you are defective and a failure, and must hide from others at all costs. This sense of failure prevents you from achieving a basic standard of acceptance, and reduced expectations of yourself or your life.

EXERCISE To understand how shame has impacted on you, make a list in your journal of how shame has affected you. Make a list of how you feel about yourself, your body and how you feel in relation to others. Think about how shame has affected your beliefs about yourself and how these have restricted your relationships with others, including your sexuality. This will guide you in identifying how shame has impacted on your sense of self.

Sharing your shame

The best antidote to shame is through human contact. Being accepted, understood and valued by someone in a non-judgemental way will enable you to release your shame. In essence, sharing your shame will enable you to come out of hiding and become more visible. To truly ease your shame you need to explore it with someone you trust at a pace that is comfortable to you.

EXERCISE In your journal make a list of trusted people that you could talk to about your sense of shame. Next, check whether you are ready to explore your shame. You will need to make sure that you have developed some control over your trauma reactions, and feel relatively stable. You must also be mindful of any potential risks involved. Make a list of the advantages and disadvantages of exploring your shame and how you can get appropriate support. You may feel it is easier to explore your shame early on in your recovery, or you may prefer to leave this near the end. When you have identified the right time, and person, for you, you will need to arrange how, where and when you can begin your exploration of the shame.

To maximise your chances of being heard, remember to check with the person whether they are happy to talk to you about your shame. This is always a good idea as it will ensure that the person is able to respond to you, rather than feel rejected. Finally, make a list of what you feel ashamed of with the most shameful at the bottom of the list and the least shameful at the top. Start by talking about the least shameful things and gradually work down the list. Exploring your shame in this order makes it less overwhelming and will build your confidence when sharing your shame.

Self-blame

As you explore your shame you will also begin to identify areas of self-blame. Like shame, it is important to recognise what you blame yourself for. If you blame yourself for not fighting back, or submitting to the abuse, it is vital that you challenge this and remember that freezing is a normal reaction to overwhelming trauma.

If you blame yourself for approaching the abuser(s), remember you did this to satisfy your need for human contact and connection NOT to be sexually abused. In addition, you may have gone back to the abuser(s) to have some control and predictability over the abuse.

Approaching the abuser(s) is a survival strategy that makes the abuse more predictable so you can prepare and steel yourself for the assault. This is a way of protecting yourself, which makes you feel less vulnerable. Similarly, if you were aroused, had an erection or orgasm during the CSA this does not mean you wanted to be sexually abused and you are not to blame.

REMEMBER If you felt aroused or experienced pleasure or orgasm during the abuse this does not mean you wanted to be sexually abused. It is simply that your body responded naturally in the presence of certain sexual touch.

Self-blame is also a way of reducing feelings of helplessness. In blaming yourself you can feel more power and control over your abuse, rather than feel helpless. While this power is illusory it does help you to feel less overwhelmed. It also helps you feel more hopeful of the future. If you take on some of the blame then that means in the future, providing you change your behaviour, you will be able to avoid being abused. While such thoughts and feelings protect you from feeling helpless, they come at a cost as the toxic effects of self-blame increase your sense of shame and self-loathing.

EXERCISE To help reduce self-blame, in your journal make a list of how you blame yourself, and what you blame yourself for. Reflect on these and evaluate them by reminding yourself that you were a child and had no choice but to submit. Your size and age would have prevented you from fighting or fleeing, leaving you no option but to freeze. You also had no knowledge or information of how to stop the abuse, or your responses to it. As in shame it will help to make a list of significant others who had a responsibility to you and who let you down. They will need to bear some blame for not protecting you.

Self-compassion is a powerful way to reduce shame and allow you to develop a more empathic view of yourself. It is vital that you practice self-compassion to reduce self-blame by recognising that what happened to you was abuse. No matter how you responded, you were a vulnerable child who was manipulated and exploited by the abuser(s). Recognising and believing this will reinforce compassion for yourself and help you to break the crippling effects of shame and self-blame.

EXERCISE To help you develop self-compassion look at photographs of yourself as a child and try to capture how you felt.

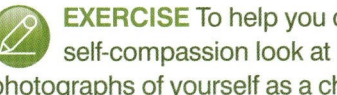

Photographs are powerful aids to recovering buried feelings and getting into contact with how you felt when you were young. If possible, try to collect a number of photographs of you, your family and the abuser(s) (if you have one) before you were abused, during the abuse and after the abuse. You could make an album of these with notes about your feelings then and now. Seeing yourself next to adults is a way of recognising how small and vulnerable you were. Next think about what you would like to say to the child, and write a letter to him or her.

Self-forgiveness

Self-forgiveness also reduces shame and self-blame. It aids recovery by accepting that you had no choice in how you reacted or responded to the abuse. You also need to forgive yourself for doing things that you thought were wrong. Remember you were a child and you did not know what to do in such a frightening or confusing situation. You may also need to forgive yourself if you have hurt others. If you have been harsh or dismissive of your non-abusing parent, your siblings or your partner, you will need to forgive yourself for not being perfect. If possible try to talk to that person and apologise for any hurt you have caused them. If this is not possible or too dangerous, send them a letter.

Forgiveness

Self-forgiveness is much more important than forgiving others, including the abuser(s). Forgiveness is a very personal thing and should only ever be decided by you. Do not let anyone tell you that you must forgive to recover. Only you can decide that. Some survivors feel relieved in forgiving their abuser(s), while others believe that CSA can never be forgiven. Yet others see forgiveness as an act of kindness to themselves rather than the abuser(s), as it permits them to let go of anger and hurt which allows them to grow. Whatever you choose will be right for YOU, and ONLY you.

⚠️ **WARNING** Forgiveness, especially of the abuser(s), is a very personal thing and can only ever be decided by you. Do not let anyone else decide this for you.

14 Managing relationships

CSA can make it extremely hard to trust others or get close to them. Fear of being hurt again or that closeness will be sexualised can lead to the avoidance of intimacy. While this has helped you to survive, it has come at a huge cost, not least aching loneliness and difficulties in relationships. This creates a paradox in which you yearn for closeness and are compelled to avoid it.

This **double bind** of desire for intimacy and fear of being suffocated can be damaging, especially if it is combined with fear of further betrayal or abuse. It will either lead you to avoid intimacy, or propel you to be too trusting, or over-intimate too quickly, making you more vulnerable to further betrayal or abuse. Both avoidance of closeness and being over-intimate can cause difficulties in relationships.

Early experiences shape how we relate to others and how much we value ourselves in relationships. You may not be consciously aware of this as it is often sensed, felt or known. As such it can easily be triggered by subtle cues that give rise to shame, anxiety or lack of worth.

The masquerade of abuse as love and affection seen in CSA makes it is difficult to know genuine love and nurturing. If you did not experience love, warmth or nurturing as a child, you will not know how to respond when this is offered. It is more than likely that such tenderness threatens pain.

The message in CSA is that your only worth in relationships is to satisfy the needs or desires of others, primarily through sex. This lack of value and respect for the whole of you can lead to wariness in your relationships, whether family, friends, partners, children, or professionals and work colleagues.

How you experience relationships

Intimacy and closeness increases resilience and is a central part of healing. Your recovery will be improved through healthy relationships and trusted support network. To help you achieve this you will need to be more aware of your experience of relationships, and identify obstacles that prevent you from enjoying intimacy and closeness. To develop close relationships you will need to explore what is meant by trust, to identify your needs and find assertive ways of expressing these.

To increase awareness of how you experience relationships and what they mean to you consider the following exercise.

EXERCISE Ask yourself the following questions and record your feelings and thoughts in your journal: What does love mean to you? What does mutual respect mean to you? How do you show that you love someone? How does it feel to receive love? How does it feel to co-operate with someone else? To what degree do you have confidence in others? How do you know you can trust someone? What evidence do you need to be ready to trust? How does it feel to trust others? How does it feel to be appreciated by others? How does it feel when you are disappointed or let down by someone? Look at your answers to these questions and reflect on them. Next ask yourself the following: What will make you feel more comfortable, safe, secure or happy in your relationships? What would you like to change or heal in your relationships?

From this exercise you can begin to identify your experience of relationships, your fears and obstacles to intimacy, and negative thoughts or feelings behind these. To reduce obstacles, you will need to challenge your negative beliefs, and replace these with more accurate ones. This will free you up to develop healthier relationships in which you enjoy greater intimacy. It will also allow you to relate more authentically in an atmosphere that is based on mutual respect and genuine care.

Relationship patterns

The previous exercise will also help identify other fears such as fear of showing vulnerability, fear of dependency, or neediness, fear of reaching out in case you are rebuffed, or fear of saying 'no' or expressing needs. To understand relationship patterns you will need to explore your fears and how these impact on your relationships. For example, do you always prioritise or anticipate the needs of others over your own needs, or do you need to constantly need to please others or find yourself reading their minds? Or do you compartmentalise your feelings so that you come across as cold and unfeeling, or have you become fiercely self-sufficient and refuse all help?

Approach and avoid

Alternatively, you might find that you veer between approaching your partner or avoiding him or her. You might find that as soon as you open up you feel compelled to shut down, or that you feel angry after you have been close, and need to reject your partner. These patterns will have been conditioned by the abuse as you learnt to prioritise your abuser(s) needs, and focused on pleasing him or her. In addition, in CSA closeness means danger, and saying 'no' or expressing needs were either punished or ignored.

Trust

The repeated betrayal in CSA leads to a basic lack of trust in self and others. Alternatively, you need to be liked, accepted and understood can lead you to trust too easily, even when there is no evidence of trustworthiness. If you have difficulties around trust, it is important to examine and challenge your thoughts and feelings about people in your life. From this you can check to what degree your trust is warranted. This is best done by plotting the degree of trust you have in them on a scale, or **continuum**.

Trust is not a static state or polarised between 'trust' and 'no trust'. It is much better seen as a spectrum, or continuum, with varying degrees of trust which can alter depending upon on the course of the relationship. To help you assess the degree of trust you have in others, try the following exercise.

EXERCISE In your journal make a list of all significant people in your life. Reflect on those you feel you can trust and those you are unsure about and those you feel you cannot trust at all. Next draw a line with 0% at one end and 100% at the other end. This represents a **continuum of trust**. Look back at your list and plot each person along this scale on the basis of the degree of trust you have in them. If they are scattered across the whole spectrum then you have a range of trusting relationships in which you do not over or under invest. If they concentrate towards the 0% end of the continuum then it is likely that you fear intimacy. If they concentrate nearer the 100% mark, then that indicates that you probably over invest or become over intimate too easily.

It can be dangerous to trust or mistrust too easily or without monitoring the evidence on which that trust is based. Look at the names on the continuum, check the evidence for your trust in them and move them along the continuum accordingly. You need to explore how you know when to trust someone and what evidence helps you in making that decision. The more aware you are of the factors that support your trust the more you will be able to assess your degree of trust.

It is helpful to review your level of trust throughout the course of a relationship, as the degree of trust is not static and will fluctuate. This can be very useful especially when there has been a betrayal of trust or when there is evidence for increased loyalty. Remember to monitor the evidence for your degree of trust in others and move people along the continuum accordingly.

> **TOP TIP** Trust is not all or nothing but exists on a spectrum of degree of trust.

Fluctuations in relationships

Avoidance of relationships not only reduces opportunities to develop trust and practice relationship skills, but prevents you from experiencing the natural fluctuations in relationships. Relationships are dynamic and their quality changes over time, with periods of closeness and periods of distance. For instance the initial thrill and excitement of attraction usually progresses into deep affection, while passion may transform into compassion and increased security and emotional intimacy. Such changes can sometimes be experienced as 'boredom' or terror as the emotional closeness intensifies.

Understanding your relationships

It is essential that when you notice any changes that you evaluate these and understand their significance. If you are feeling bored ask yourself if this really is boredom, or is it that you are unfamiliar with security and close intimacy. Alternatively, if you start to experience fear explore what this represents before ending the relationship prematurely. In addition you might find that what initially attracted you to your partner, or friend may repel you when the relationship is under stress. Suddenly the very thing that attracted you, such as their independence, serenity or attentiveness, will feel like distance, unemotional or fussing.

The more you understand the rhythm of relationships the more you will be able to accept that all relationships, even healthy ones, are messy at times. Even in healthy relationships ruptures can occur and, more importantly, be repaired. This will help you to be more tolerant and realistic in your expectations of others and yourself in relationships.

Relationship skills

Your lack of experience in relationships can also lead to a lack of confidence and the necessary social skills needed to get close to people. Developing your social skills through use of body language, eye contact and smiling can all help you to interact more easily with others. To help you acquire these try to observe people who are socially skilled and are good at initiating relationships.

These could be friends or colleagues, or fictional characters on television, in films or in books. Look at how they interact with others. What sort of facial expressions do they use, how often do they smile and how long do they hold eye contact? To help you in making conversation, listen to what friendly phrases they use to start and maintain a conversation? Make a note of these in your journal and try to adopt these.

It is a good idea to practice these skills first with a trusted friend or colleague so that they become easier and more automatic when you try them out. They can then give you advice or constructive feedback before entering more difficult social situations. You may also need to learn and practice being more assertive (see **Four stages of assertiveness** on page 110). This can also be learnt by observing others being assertive and seeing what works and what doesn't.

Identifying your needs

Before you can be assertive you will need to feel comfortable about expressing your feelings and needs in relationships. This can be hard if these were consistently ignored, or you were punished for expressing them in the past. You may not be in contact with your needs, or feel entitled to have any.

Before you can express your needs you will have to identify them.

 EXERCISE Think about your needs and make a list of them. If you are stuck, then consider some of the following: the need to feel safe, to feel loved, to feel respected and to feel comfortable about showing your vulnerability without fear or shame. Also important is the need to be able to say 'no' without being rejected or humiliated, and the need to be listened to. Try to add any other needs that are important to you. Look at the list and think about what you can do to meet these.

Expressing your needs

Once you have identified your needs you will need to find a way of expressing them. This needs to be done assertively, which can be difficult initially as you may have no role models for what it means to be assertive. Being assertive is the complete opposite of the manipulation, threat and aggression the abuser(s) used to get what he or she wanted. This means it will be very unfamiliar to you, and make it hard to do so.

Assertiveness must not be confused with being selfish, insensitive or hostile. It is a sophisticated social skill in which there is a balance between respect for the self and respect for others. To be assertive means being respectful of the rights of others while keeping your own respect and rights in mind. It means communicating in a non-aggressive, non-manipulative and proactive way whereby you maintain respect for your needs and balance this with what is fair, reasonable and respectful of others.

Assertiveness does not demand that needs are met but is way of expressing these in the hope that they can be met in negotiation with the other person. This may mean reaching a compromise in which both parties feel respected. The important ingredients are honesty in stating your needs and being respectful to yourself and others. While it helps to be assertive when face to face with the person, this is not always possible. If this is the case, then consider writing a letter, phoning or acting through a trusted third party.

Four stages of assertiveness

To be assertive you need to work through four stages. Firstly you have to **decide precisely what it is you want or need**. Secondly you need to **decide what is reasonable and fair**. This will help in stage three which is to **generate a reasonable proposal**, which includes room for compromise. Finally you have to **consider and state the consequences** if your proposal is not properly considered or ignored.

Once you have gone through these stages, you will need to practise and rehearse your newly acquired assertion skills until they come more naturally. It helps to rehearse these with a trusted friend or in front of a mirror until you feel more confident.

Opposition to assertiveness

While most people respond well to the communication of feelings and needs, it is worth noting that some people refuse to acknowledge assertion. Instead they choose to interpret this as opposition or defiance, especially if it threatens the status quo or long established ways of interacting. It helps to be prepared for potential opposition no matter how assertive you are especially if you are currently in an abusive relationship. In this case, you must ensure you are safe before approaching your partner.

Some of this opposition may be direct and explicit, while some may be much more subtle in terms of disapproval, emotional manipulation or redirection of blame. To manage any opposition you will need to stand your ground and restate your case assertively, sometimes several times.

Remember, while it is understandable that others may not want to accept your feelings or needs, this does not invalidate them. It certainly shouldn't become a reason to stop you from expressing yourself. Try to stay calm, and repeat your feelings or needs. If the other person remains negative in their responses to you, you may need to accept that they are being unreasonable.

If they remain unfair, try to manipulate you or end the discussion try not interpret this as failure. It clearly demonstrates that the person you are talking to is not able to respect you, your feelings or your needs. Remind yourself that the point of assertion is not demanding that your needs be met, but that you are expressing yourself in the hope of being heard. If your request or need is met that is a bonus. However if it is not then you can still feel proud that you at least respected yourself in expressing your need.

WARNING Some people, especially those who have, or had, power over you will not respond well to assertion. They may punish you to bring you back in line. Be careful and remember to stay safe.

Asserting yourself can be difficult and taxing and can prompt losses, such as the loss of relationships that are no longer tenable. It is important to pace yourself in developing assertiveness and seek extra support if necessary. You could also go on assertiveness training, or work on these skills in your counselling.

Relationship ground rules

Once you feel comfortable expressing your feelings and needs, you can begin to work on setting ground rules for your relationships. Make a list of the ground rules and boundaries that ensure that your needs are met. As you write them down you may be plagued by objections about expressing these such as *'People won't like me'*, *'I will be rejected'*, *'I am being selfish'* or *'I will feel guilty'*. Such objections while common need to be challenged to help you overcome them and begin to discuss them.

Boundaries and ground rules help to build or rebuild trust which will allow you to relate more authentically. With healthy boundaries in place you can stop anticipating the needs of others, mind reading, or taking responsibility for the feelings, thoughts and behaviour of others. This will help you to stop prioritising others at cost to yourself.

Healthy boundaries will also enable you to distinguish between genuinely nurturing and nourishing relationships and those that are forceful and controlling. It will empower you to monitor the quality of your relationships and manage any difficulties more effectively rather than avoiding intimacy. Most importantly, in expressing your feelings, needs and communicating these more effectively you will be able to develop intimacy without feeling threatened or suffocated.

Listening to each other, talking honestly, expressing feelings, needs and desires will allow for more satisfying relationships which are built upon trust and mutual respect. If you feel you could benefit from extra support in helping you in your relationship you may consider contacting Relate (see **Resources** on page 176) who offer counselling to couples.

15 Managing sexual difficulties

CSA can give rise to a range of sexual difficulties which can be distressing and affect sexual relationships. While some survivors experience little or no difficulties, others feel that their sexual lives have been forever damaged. The spectrum of sexual difficulties can range from avoidance of all sexual activities through to indiscriminate sexual encounters.

You might avoid sexual intimacy because fear, mistrust or sexual experiences are physically or emotionally painful. Or you might experience phobic reactions to certain parts of the body or specific sexual acts. You may also experience physical complications such as pain on penetration or erectile difficulties which can fuel a fear of failure and sense of inadequacy.

Alternatively you may suffer from flashbacks or intrusive memories during sex, even when in a loving relationship. Sex might also be so tainted by shame or guilt that you cannot experience any pleasure. Or you might avoid sex altogether and only engage in compulsive masturbation in which you experience neither pleasure or satisfaction.

In the case of indiscriminate sexual behaviour, you may have had numerous sexual partners yet experience little or no sexual pleasure. This may be due to a need to prove that you have not been sexually damaged, or a way of getting your need for affection met. You could also be trying to empower yourself by being predatory or in control of your sexual encounters. Sometimes, such behaviour is simply due to not being able to say 'no' to someone who wants to have sex with you. This can make you vulnerable to sexually abusive relationships in which love and hurt become intertwined and confused.

To manage sexual difficulties you will need to rebuild a safe sexual foundation and learn to take sensual pleasure in your body. To help you achieve this you will need to identify any myths about sex you may have and to challenge these. From this you can develop a greater understanding and knowledge of sex and sexual arousal. This will help you to recognise the importance of a safe and healthy relationship in which to develop sexual trust.

The quality of your sexual relationship will be enhanced if you can communicate sexual fears as well as your sexual desires without shame or fear of rejection. This can help you to break old associations to CSA. As you begin to feel more comfortable about intimacy you can reclaim your body and your sexuality.

REMEMBER To reclaim your body and sexuality it is critical to go at your own pace.

Sexual myths

Sexual myths influence beliefs around sex, sexuality and direct sexual behaviour. Some of these myths may have been conditioned during the CSA or imposed by your abuser(s) to distort reality and obtain power and control over you. The first step in reclaiming your sexuality is to become more conscious and aware of the myths that influence your beliefs about sex.

EXERCISE Here is a list of **common sexual myths** as reported by survivors. You may have others you wish to include. Look at these and identify those that apply to you and those that have affected your sexual relationships. Discuss them with a trusted friend or your partner and try to challenge them with alternative or more accurate beliefs.

- Any physical contact inevitably leads to sex

- If you are aroused you must want to have sex

- All cuddles are a prelude to sex

- Men always want and must be ready for sex, and if they don't they are inadequate

- If your partner does not have sex with you then they don't love you or find you unattractive

- To have sex necessitates an erection

- Sex is only sex when penetration takes place

- Once you are sexually aroused you lose control and have to have sex

- Men and women have to have orgasms to enjoy sex

- Sex is only satisfying if both partners orgasm at the same time

- Once orgasm or ejaculation occurs sex is over

- Lots of sex is the only way to a healthy relationship

- You must agree to sex whenever your partner wants to

- You are not allowed to say 'no' to sex

- To be sexual you must be young, beautiful or have a good body

- CSA has made you gay or lesbian.

To reclaim your sexuality you will to need challenge these myths and replace them with more accurate knowledge. Such knowledge will improve your understanding of sex and sexuality improve the quality of your sexual relationships. You will be able to reverse the sexual naivety imposed by your abuser(s) and take more control over your sexual responses. CSA denied you the natural discovery of sexual likes and dislikes, wants or desires. It also distorted the role of love and care in sexual relationships by entwining hurt and pain with pleasure. In essence it dictated what you should and should not feel, and created a pattern for all future sexual relationships.

Understanding the impact of CSA on you

The pleasure of physical contact through hugs has become confused and tainted with the demands of being sexual, and to satisfy someone else's needs. CSA also distorts your understanding of the nature of sexual relationships, and the ebb and flow of feeling sexually attractive or attracted to your partner. It also affects your ability to regulate sexual behaviour, being able to say 'no' without feeling guilty or ashamed, and the frequency with which you should have sex.

The betrayal of the body

You may have felt betrayed by your body if you felt pleasure during the CSA. Yet you may not realise that your abuser(s) most likely performed specific sexual acts on you to deliberately arouse. By feeling pleasure you will have blamed yourself believing that you wanted the sexual contact. This is a clever way for your abuser(s) to shift responsibility for the abuse on you and thereby reducing the risk of disclosure. The shame of being sexually aroused, or having an orgasm, further reduces the likelihood of disclosure.

Bodily responses

It is important to realise that if you had an erection, or became lubricated, that these are natural responses in the presence of sexual touch. Erections can be involuntary and happen in a variety of situations, including fear and stress. Similarly, vaginal lubrication in females is an automatic biological reaction which acts as a natural form of protection from tissue damage. Neither of these necessarily indicate sexual desire or arousal. Such reactions can occur for non-sexual reasons much like nipples that become erect not just during sexual arousal but also due to fear or cold.

The sexual arousal cycle

Once the sexual arousal system has been activated, and in the presence of continued stimulation, it will naturally tend to lead to orgasm. If you experienced involuntary orgasms or ejaculation during CSA this does not mean that you wanted or encouraged the sexual encounter. It certainly does not mean that you are responsible or to blame for CSA.

REMEMBER Your body is biologically programmed to become aroused, experience pleasure and orgasm in the presence of sexual stimulation.

You are not dirty, sinful or a whore. Remember your body responded to the sexual stimulation and not the person. These normal physical responses were exploited by your abuser(s) to make you feel bad and ashamed in order to reduce the risk of disclosure.

REMEMBER Your body responded to the sexual stimulation and not the person.

Sexual arousal and sexual desire

It is vital that you distinguish between sexual arousal and sexual desire. Sexual arousal and sexual desire are two quite separate things; you can be sexually aroused without the desire to be sexual, or engage in a sexual experience. Thus sexual arousal is an appropriate response to sexual stimulation. It is the abuser's sexual activity with you as a child that is inappropriate.

Physical pain during sex

Physical pain during sex may be fear related as you involuntarily tense up to protect yourself, which can lead to further anxiety and sexual difficulties. You may believe that such pain is as a result of physical damage to external or internal sexual organs. If you have such fears you could allay these by having a medical examination with a sensitive specialist. In addition, if you have anatomical concerns such as the shape or size of your penis, breasts, clitoris or vagina, it is worth talking these through too. While most survivors do not sustain physical damage or deformities due to CSA it is important to take your concerns seriously and seek medical advice.

TOP TIP If you are concerned about physical or sexual damage it is worth seeking advice from a sensitive medical practitioner.

A reflex reaction to fear is muscular tension which can lead to pain when attempting sexual intercourse. This is called **vaginismus** whereby the muscles contract upon attempting penetration, making it virtually impossible to insert a penis. While lubricants can help, it is more beneficial in the long term if you can learn to reduce your fears and learn to relax. Men who have extremely tight foreskins, which make erections and sexual intercourse painful, are also advised to seek medical advice.

Emotional reactions

Fear can also affect the emotional temperature of sexual relationships. You may feel overwhelmed by powerful feelings during sex such as terror, shame, humiliation or anger that you fear you cannot contain. You may experience flashbacks or intrusive memories during sexual stimulation which can lead to 'tuning out', or **dissociation**. This is because sexual intimacy triggers the same bodily sensations as during the CSA which propel you back to the abuse experience.

Your terror, anxiety or anger in turn triggers a range of defensive reactions such as detachment, withdrawal or aggression. This can be frightening to both you and your partner especially if the link to CSA has not been made. It does not mean that you do not love and care for your partner, it is a conditioned response as a result of CSA. In linking such responses to CSA, and identifying the triggers that induce fear, anger or dissociation, you can begin to take control of them.

EXERCISE To identify triggers and sensory cues, think about all the cues that were present during CSA and make a list of these. Try to include as many of the sensory cues as possible. List all the smells you associate with the abuse such as body odours or breath, the smell of tobacco or alcohol, semen or any other ones. Next identify as many sounds as you can remember, such as the abuser's voice or any other voices, the radio, TV or music. Then list all that you could see during the abuse and the quality of the light or darkness. You also need to identify any tactile sensation such as how the abuser(s) touched you. Was it tender and gentle or rough and aggressive? Were the abuser's hands soft or abrasive? What body parts did he or she touch, which parts did you have to touch and how did that feel? You also need to list any tastes associated with the CSA such as semen or other bodily secretions. Lastly, try to identify positions your body was placed in and the preferred position of the abuser(s).

Changing sensory cues

Once you have identified these sensory cues you can erase or replace them with new sensory cues that are associated with your present loving relationship. Talk to your partner and explore how you can make changes. If possible vary your sexual positions, introduce pleasant smells such as body oil or lotions to offset the unpleasant smells and to change the experience of being touched. Try to find new ways to experience pleasure that does not repeat the sexual stimulation used by the abuser(s).

Vary the light by using scented candles, and the sound by talking in a loving way, or by being silent, or other sounds such as music up or down. If the CSA always took place in the bedroom, experiment by having sex in different settings to see if that makes a difference. You could also experiment with who initiates sexual contact, or by taking more control of the process to offset the abuse experience.

The more you experiment with different sensory cues the more you will be able to erase the old associations and reduce any defence mechanisms. As you feel more pleasure in your body, you may want to experiment more. You might increase your sexual pleasure through fantasy, looking at or reading erotic material, or using sexual aids. Do not do this if you were forced to do this during the CSA. Changing sensory cues can really help you to reclaim your sexuality, and allow you feel pleasure for pleasure's sake without feeling guilty, dirty or ashamed.

What it means to be sexual

To further reclaim your sexuality you need to know what being sexual means to you. CSA prevented you from exploring your own sexuality and as a result you will know how to perform without necessarily feeling sexual. To discover what being sexual means to you, you need to explore your feelings about your body, and identify what gives you pleasure.

 EXERCISE Take some time to reflect on what being sexual means to you. What do you enjoy the most about being sexual? What do you like the least? What makes you feel comfortable or uncomfortable? What are your fears around sex and sexual relationships? What is the purpose of sex for you? Try to answer these, and any other questions you have, and list your responses in your journal. Reflect on these and record what you would like to change and what would help you to make those changes.

Your feelings about your body can have considerable effect on your feelings about being sexual. If you hate your body or the body parts that have been fetishised by the abuser(s), this will impact significantly on your sexuality. Negative feelings, confusion about your body, or lack of control over bodily responses can lead to shame and guilt.

Body shame

If you feel ashamed of your body you will tend to want to hide your body covering up or disguising your appearance. This includes wearing dull or baggy clothing, putting on excess weight, or disfigurement to ward off sexual advances. You may also neglect personal hygiene to repel others and to avoid physical closeness.

Alternatively you may wear layers of make up to compensate for feeling unattractive, or dress in an overtly sexual manner. This is an attempt to hide feeling asexual or to achieve a sexual identity through dress. You might also diet to excess, or starve yourself to reduce breast size or curves that remind you of sexuality. To achieve this you might binge and purge food as a way of recreating the bodily conflict of pleasure and pain of CSA.

If you are a male survivor you may body build to excess to compensate for feeling vulnerable and to protect against any future abuse. Females may also exercise to excess to gain control over a body they feel betrayed them during the CSA. To enable you to enjoy and take pleasure in your body try the following exercise.

EXERCISE To explore how to enjoy your body, think about what could give you pleasure. This can be through affection through being held, cuddled or stroked in a non-sexual way. Or it could be being wrapped in a warm, fluffy towel, splashing in water, feeling air on your skin or being naked without being sexualised. You could also find pleasure through running, swimming, dancing, skipping or any physical activity which allows you to feel in control of your body and develop bodily trust. Further sources of pleasure include dressing up, wearing soft, sensual clothing, taking pride in your appearance and receiving compliments without feeling shame or fear of sexual abuse.

Reflect on how you could start to take pleasure in your body by allowing yourself to engage in some of these things on a regular basis. You can also gain pleasure from nourishing your body in taking care of it by eating healthily and exercising regularly. You could also take more pleasure in your appearance by wearing soft, sensual clothing and wearing scent. You can nourish your skin by applying scented oil or lotion after bathing, or having a regular relaxing massage.

Sensate focus

In addition to this you can begin to explore your body and its responses through specific exercise such as **sensate focus**. This can be done individually or with a partner. Sensate focus is designed for you to get to know your body through self-exploration, or mutual exploration with a trusted partner. You can start by looking at yourself in the mirror and make a note of what you like and dislike about your body.

This is followed by stroking yourself and noticing how that feels. Initially this involves stroking your head, hands and feet and noting down any feelings or bodily sensations. Once you feel comfortable stroking these areas you can start to stroke your legs, arms, neck and upper body. Gradually you can work up to stroking the breast and genital area, remembering to write down your feelings and sensations. When you feel comfortable with this you can stimulate the genitals by rhythmically stroking your penis or clitoris, or inserting a finger into the vagina.

It is essential that you take your time to explore your body at a pace that is comfortable for you. If you feel in any way uncomfortable, anxious or upset, stop and try again another day. It is best if you practice sensate focus over several weeks rather than rush through it. It is also important to reflect on your feelings and note which sensations are pleasurable and which are uncomfortable as this will help you to identify what gives you pleasure.

Sensate focus with your partner can improve the communication between you so that you know how to please each other. When practising sensate focus with your partner you each need to take turns to touch and stroke each other. As you do this it is helpful to tell each other how the touch feels and what is pleasurable and what is not. It is essential when doing this that you agree that either partners can stop at any point.

To get the most benefit from sensate focus you also need to agree not to have sex throughout the period of exploration no matter how aroused. This ensures safety and increases communication of the full range of sensations. Giving each other pleasure without sex can help you to know how to please each other non-sexually, how to talk to each other and discover more creative ways of expressing your sensuality as well as your sexuality.

 WARNING **If you practice sensate focus with a partner make sure that they are truly willing and committed to this and that they agree to the boundaries.**

Mood and your sexual relationship

Your sexual relationship is also influenced by your mood. Stress and unresolved anger can reduce your libido which can impact on your desire to have sex as well your arousal and erectile difficulties. For women, your monthly hormonal cycle plays a significant role in enhancing or reducing you libido. Unresolved anger, conflicts and arguments all pose considerable obstacles to a healthy sexual relationship.

Lack of control and unpredictability can also become a problem as this is reminiscent of the abuse. You may prefer to have some sense advance warning of when to have sex so that you mentally prepare yourself and get in the right mood. A degree of advance warning may feel more comfortable rather than feeling it is imposed upon you. While this reduces spontaneity it does mean that you have some of the control over when to have sex.

Alternatively you may resort to alcohol to reduce sexual fears and anxiety as alcohol can reduce any inhibitions you may have. While a small amount of alcohol can help you to relax, remember to be mindful that too much alcohol can affect both your performance and your experience of pleasure.

To enhance sexual mood, desire and arousal you need to **feel safe and be free of any interruptions**. This is necessary especially if you feared and yet desired interruption when you were being abused. If you cannot fully relax you will find it difficult to enjoy the sexual experience .

Sexual trust is another necessary component of a healthy sexual relationship. In order to enable sexual trust you need to have clear boundaries and ground rules. This ensures safety and reduces feeling demeaned or humiliated. This can only be achieved with good communication wherein you are free to express your needs to feel safe.

EXERCISE Take some time to think about your needs to feel safe in your sexual relationship. If this is difficult it may be easier to think of what needs were not met during the CSA as this can highlight what you do need. The most common needs include the need to feel loved, to feel equally in control, to feel able to say 'no' or stop having sex if uncomfortable, and the need to feel fine with not always wanting penetrative sex. Male survivors need to feel accepted and valued despite occasional erectile difficulties, premature ejaculation or inability to perform. Most importantly, you need to feel that you are valued for who you are and not just as sexual objects. Remember to add any other specific needs to this list. Once you have compiled your list of needs you can express and discuss them with your partner, to establish mutually agreed ground rules.

The more you can talk to your partner and express your sexual needs without fear of upsetting your partner, being hurtful, or rejecting, the more you will experience sexual trust. This will also allow you to set limits, boundaries and ground rules in which you can express your desire, or say 'no' without fearing negative consequences.

Ground rules

Ground rules necessary for a healthy sexual relationship must include regularly telling each other that you love each other, paying each other compliments and permitting each other to initiate or stop sex. It is vital that either partner can say 'no' without feeling hurt, rejected or humiliated. A particularly important ground rule is that hugs or cuddles do not always need to lead to sex but are merely an expression of affection. In discussing and establishing mutually agreed ground rules you will significantly improve the quality of your sexual relationship.

If you find it too terrifying to have sex with another person you may need to put sexual intimacy on hold. You may find it easier to engage in sexual fantasy through the use of the internet, or by watching or reading erotic material and masturbation. This must always be a choice and should not be judged by you or anyone else. You must not let yourself be pressurised to enter a sexual relationship if you are not ready for it.

While many sexual difficulties can be worked though by yourself, or with your partner, you can always seek extra support through counselling or psychosexual therapy. If you have any specific concerns, or feel compelled to masturbate excessively with no feeling of sexual pleasure or release despite orgasm or ejaculation, you may need to consider seeking specialist support.

16 Managing grief and loss

CSA and trauma is inextricably linked to loss, both in the past and present. You may not however feel entitled to grieve due to self-blame, shame and negative self-beliefs. The losses sustained in CSA occur across all dimensions including physical and psychological losses, as well as spiritual losses. In order to mourn losses, your firstly have to identify your losses.

Common losses associated with CSA include actual and symbolic losses such as loss of childhood, loss of protective parent(s), loss of a nurturing family, as well as the loss of self, self-esteem and self-worth, and loss of control and autonomy. Loss of trust in self and others as well as loss of belief that the world can be a benign place are also common.

CSA also results in the loss of well-being, loss of control over your body, loss of continuity or belongingness, the loss of healthy relationships and the belief in a better future. Spiritual losses cluster around loss of faith and hope, and, in the case of clerical abuse, loss of belief in your religious beliefs. Current and future losses include loss of hope in restoring damaged family relationships or the yearned for relationship with the abuser(s) or non-abusing parent(s). These losses will also need to be mourned.

Obstacles to grieving

If you are haunted by self-blame and negative self-thoughts this will present a major obstacle to grieving as it prevents you from legitimising the CSA. Before starting the grieving process you will need to work through shame, self-blame and negative self-beliefs to fully acknowledge the impact of CSA has had on you. This needs to be supported by self-compassion and empathy in order to permit the grieving process. This may present a number of challenges as the grief process is rarely straightforward or continuous.

Phases of grief

As you begin to grieve you will find yourself weaving in and out of various phases of grief. These tend to include periods of numbness, yearning for what is lost and preoccupation with your loss. In addition, loss and grieving gives rise to many feelings, not just sadness. You might also experience feelings of guilt, anger, shame and jealousy. These are all normal and need to be worked through before you can accept the loss and recover.

Built up grief forms a reservoir which when you start to grieve, can feel overwhelming. For this reason it is vital that you pace yourself and make sure that you nurture yourself throughout the process. You need to take your time to work through the range of losses and increase self-nurturing activities. Over time the aching pain of loss subsides but there may always be a nub of sadness.

If built up grief is not released it can turn into what is called **traumatic grief**. Traumatic grief is grief that has been prolonged over many years. This is usually accompanied by chronic clinical depression, persistent sadness and deep sense of hopelessness. This can severely undermine your capacity to function and engage in life. If you experience persistent traumatic grief that overwhelms and incapacitates you, you need to seek additional support through counselling.

WARNING If you experience persistent traumatic grief that overwhelms and incapacitates you, you need to seek additional support through counselling.

There are a number of exercises that can help you to grieve and you may find some of these helpful. Remember only attempt those that you feel could be useful and to pace yourself. Before starting the grieving process you will need to identify the range of losses you have experienced.

EXERCISE To identify the range of losses, think about and make a list of all the losses you have experienced. This could be recorded in two lists. One list can represent losses in the past while the other represents losses in the present or that you face during your recovery. Remember that many of the losses associated with CSA are symbolic such as the loss of innocence, loss of childhood or loss of self-discovery of sexuality. Some are still present now such as loss of control over your body, loss of well-being or belief in a future without pain or abuse. Look at your lists and reflect on what feelings emerge and note these. Next explore on how you have managed feelings of loss in the past. Did you avoid your feelings or did you try to connect with them, did you reach out to others or did you withdraw from them? How you would like to be in the future?

REMEMBER Give yourself space to grieve and to really acknowledge your losses and sadness.

Understanding the impact of loss

As you identify each loss, try to notice your thoughts and feelings and link these to the loss. This will give you a deeper understanding of how the loss affected you in the past, and how it continues to affect you in the present.

EXERCISE Look at your list of losses and make two columns in your journal, one headed *'Things I miss'* and one headed *'Things I don't miss'*. Enter your losses under these headings to help you identify those losses that still hurt and those losses that you have let go of and do not miss. It is also important to consider any losses you might sustain whilst making changes during your recovery and to grieve these. These can also be divided into those things that you will miss and those you will not miss.

To help you in the grieving process you need to mark your losses by performing a memorial ritual to honour the loss and your grief. This can be performed for each loss individually or you could devote a specific period of time to honour a number of losses. Try the exercises below.

ACTIVITY Gather together photographs or clippings of both sad and nice memories. Put the photographs in your memory book or album and write or make notes alongside these. If you are making a memory box put in things that remind you of your losses. This could include images of childhood, a favourite childhood book, or film, a stuffed toy, or reminders of a childhood hobby or collection. Write down any associated thoughts or feelings in your memory book and put it into your memory box.

Keep your memory book or box in a place where you can easily find it and look at it whenever you feel sad and are in contact with your losses. You can also make specific time to grieve such as in the following activity.

ACTIVITY Set aside a specific time as a **'night to remember'** to grieve away from any distractions. Light some scented candles, or spray your favourite scent or aftershave to ground you. You might use an aromatic scent that is commonly used in commemoration ceremonies such as sage, sandalwood, or rosemary or burn incense to create the right atmosphere. This is not a good idea if such scents are associated with the CSA, such as in clerical abuse. You might also put on some celebratory music to accompany the ceremony. Take out and look at your memory book or memory box and add things to these. You might consider writing a special letter to the source of the loss such as the young child, the innocent self or the lost parts of the self. This letter can then be 'sent' by burying or burning it and scattering the ashes.

Memorial ceremonies

This exercise can be adapted and be performed as a group memorial in which each person writes or says a personal goodbye. Alternatively you could write a message on a balloon and release this. As you watch the balloon rise and drift away recognise your acceptance and letting go of the loss. A variation on this is the 'river of life' ceremony in which you make a small paper boat in which to place your message regarding the loss. Place a tea light into the boat and light the candle. Then set the boat afloat in a small river or stream and watch it float away. You could also put a flower or other significant, symbolic object into the boat with your message.

Expressing your grief

Whichever ritual or ceremony you use, remember to record your grief journey by writing about your experiences. Remember to express the full range of your feelings including anger and tears. If you have difficulty releasing either anger or tears you will need to explore your beliefs around the expression of emotions and how much that has been shaped by the CSA.

Often tears are seen as a weakness, especially in males, or were ignored or not permitted when you were a child.

Similarly, you may fear expressing your anger or vulnerability because you were punished or humiliated for that in childhood. It will help to explore any negative beliefs around crying, expressing anger or vulnerability and to reassess these so they can be expressed. Remember that while these messages originated in childhood they do not have to persist in adulthood as they can sabotage your recovery.

EXERCISE To explore your beliefs around crying, you will need to reflect on what messages shaped your beliefs about crying. What were the messages in your family around crying? How were you made to feel when you cried – weak, pathetic, vulnerable or contemptuous? Were you punished when you cried or did it increase the level of cruelty? Perhaps not crying and detaching took the pain away. If you are a male were you taught that boys or men should not cry no matter how much pain they feel? Alternatively, are you afraid that if you cry you will lose control or not be able to stop?

List whichever messages apply to you and check the evidence for these messages. You will also need to consider the benefits of crying such as the release of sadness, hurt and pain and how it aids healing. Crying is known to improve well-being, and reduce blood pressure and heart rate. If you are comfortable with crying you could do the same exercise to identify beliefs about the expression of anger and vulnerability.

REMEMBER You cannot force tears, so allow yourself to cry naturally and allow yourself to reclaim this human response to sadness and loss.

Once you have identified your losses you can begin to explore what was missing in your childhood and is still absent in adulthood. While you can never replace these losses you can begin to compensate for any deficits by ensuring that these no longer persist in your current everyday life. For instance if you were too terrified to play or not allowed to have fun, give yourself permission to have fun or to play now. If you lacked nurturing, you can make sure that you are nurtured now.

EXERCISE To reclaim losses, look at your list of losses and highlight those losses that you can replace. In identifying those things that were missing in childhood you will be able to consider how you can balance them now. Make a list of the losses that can be reclaimed and how you can introduce these into your life now. For example, if your losses include lack of security it is important to find sources of safety and security in the present. If you avoided people in the past you could develop friendships now. If you never felt 'special' you could ensure that you do things now that make you feel special.

If you felt psychologically orphaned as a child you can rebalance this by building a good support network now. This will reinstate a sense of belongingness by creating a new 'family' in which you are respected, nurtured and loved. While these can never make up for the actual losses incurred, they can go some way to improving the quality of your life in the present and future.

Readjusting to the world

Recognising and mourning your losses will help you to relegate the CSA to the past and allow you to readjust to the world now and move forward. Although your abuse experiences will always remain a part of your life history, they will no longer dominate or control who you are. They will merely be a part of your life experiences rather than identifying the whole you. In this you will become freer to move forward and embrace your future without being haunted by the terror, pain and fear of abuse.

To celebrate moving forward you could honour your losses by making something that symbolises your journey of recovery. This could be a painting, a sculpture, a poem or song. You could also consider painting a commemorative plate, plaque or a memory tile which symbolises your journey of recovery.

Part three
Rebuilding your life

17 Restoring your reality and trust in yourself

To restore your reality means learning to trust yourself again. In trusting yourself you can begin to trust others. The more you understand how CSA has affected you the better you will be able to see how this prevented you from listening to yourself. This will help you to get in touch with how you feel. Once you are no longer on red alert, or in survival mode, you will be able to gauge how you feel and think. Then you can stop being influenced by the expectations of others. This will allow you to reject other people's judgements of you and to value your own judgement.

Inner experiencing

A useful way to restore trust in your intuition is to listen to your **inner experiencing**, or gut instinct. Do not be forced into making any instant decisions and take time to reflect on what you truly feel or think. Remember it is okay to say *'I don't know but will get back to you.'* Anyone who rushes you into instant answers or decisions is not respecting your right to reflect in your own time. If you have any doubts this means you are not sure and need to think about what is being said or requested. It is essential that you listen to your doubts and take them seriously. The following exercise will help you to be more skilled in this by developing your internal gauge.

 EXERCISE Developing your internal gauge. To develop your internal gauge, imagine it as ruler with a scale of one to ten, with one being very unsure and ten being very sure. Whenever you have doubts about something, try to plot the degree of doubt on the scale. If you are unsure you need to listen to the doubts before making any decision. Make a list of the doubts and reflect on them by asking yourself what is the evidence for or against them. This will allow you to move the doubts along the scale and help you to decide what is best for you.

 REMEMBER Doubts are inner signals that you are not sure. You need to listen to them before making any decision.

Inner wisdom

The more you listen to yourself the more you will be able to develop your own inner value system and inner wisdom. Using your inner wisdom, or **internal locus of evaluation**, will restore your trust in yourself rather than be influenced by others. This will help rebuild your self-esteem and help you make more positive choices that are right for you.

As you start to listen to and trust yourself more you will find that you are more able to be in contact with your needs, rather than focusing on the needs of others. This will free you up to express your needs and find ways of meeting these rather than anticipating and trying to meet the needs of others. In this you will find it easier to distinguish between what feels right for you. This will lead to what is known as an **internal locus of control** in which you feel you are in control of your thoughts, feelings and actions.

In trusting yourself more you will be able to accept and value yourself more, including your personal qualities. This will help to repair your self-esteem and develop a self-image that is based on a realistic evaluation of yourself rather than that imposed by others. The exercise below can help with this.

EXERCISE In your journal make a list of which personal qualities you admire in others. Look at this list and note how many of these also apply to you. Make sure you add others that you know you have. Talk to a trusted friend who may also have some qualities to add to the list. As you reflect on your personal qualities try to gauge to what extent you accept or reject these in your daily life. Make sure you regularly remind yourself of these qualities and thereby change your self-image. You could do this by including your personal qualities in your cookie jar (see **Rewarding yourself** on page 42).

Restoring self-reliance

Restoring trust in yourself allows you to become more self-reliant. This will reduce your dependency on others who may let you down or betray your trust. Such self-reliance must not be confused with fierce self-sufficiency which is really a protection from others. This self-reliance is based on knowing that you can trust yourself in identifying, expressing and meeting your needs without depending on others to decide for you. It also means that you can choose when to ask for help or feedback from others and when to be independent. Ultimately, this provides you with more choices rather than feeling controlled by others.

Initially it might be hard to become more self-reliant as it means making changes that can produce anxiety and fears. To manage these remember to pace yourself and to monitor your progress. Keeping a record of situations in which you have shown increased trust in yourself acts as a powerful reminder of your recovery. Remember to include both positive and negative things that have happened, and how you managed these to give you direct evidence of your accomplishments.

It also helps to record what you have learnt about yourself and how this has increased your self-confidence. With practice and regular monitoring you will be able to balance your internal and external reality based on your own judgement and evaluation. In addition, as you trust yourself more you will be able to begin to trust others and trust in a better future.

18 Expressing your feelings and needs

Once you are more in touch with your inner experiencing you will be able to identify and express your feelings and needs without guilt or shame. Many survivors are unable to express their feelings or needs as they fear being humiliated or punished. You may fear showing your vulnerability in case you are exploited or abused again, or you may avoid expressing negative feelings in case you are rejected. Alternatively you may have learnt that you are not entitled to express your feelings or needs and therefore have no idea how to go about expressing yourself.

You might also have difficulty expressing your feelings or needs because you are out of touch with them or because you have learnt to ignore them. If you believe your feelings are dangerous you learn to shut them down. This can include negative as well as positive feelings. In disconnecting from your feelings you begin to live only half a life.

As you begin to recover you will find that feelings that have been shut down for many years will start to resurface. This can be terrifying initially as you may not be confident in expressing them. Before you can express your feelings you will need to explore them so that you can identify them more clearly.

Write down how you feel

A good way of doing this is to write down how you feel about your abuse, the abuser(s) and any other significant people in your life. This can be done in the form of a letter to either yourself or you as the child, or the person you have feelings about. This could be your abuser(s), the non-abusing parent, your sibling(s) or any other significant person in your life. It is important not to censor yourself as you will not send the letter.

In writing down how you feel you will be able to recognise the full range of your feelings and needs. Once you have done this you will be able to consider ways to express them. This can be difficult initially, especially if these are conflicting or contradictory.

Expressing anger

One emotion that might be hard to express is anger. Anger is a healthy emotion that helps you to protect and assert yourself. However, if it is ignored, bottled up, misdirected or expressed inappropriately it can become destructive. The healthy expression of anger can be liberating and promote growth which is why it is important to recognise your anger and to express it.

REMEMBER Anger is a healthy emotion that helps you to protect and assert yourself.

EXERCISE In your journal write down how you manage and express your anger. To help you ask yourself the following questions: What do you usually do with your feelings of anger? Do you express anger through anxiety or fear, hunger, the need for a drink or a cigarette, or do you become silent and withdrawn? Where do you direct your anger, at the source, or do you direct it at others who are not responsible for the anger? Do you express your anger openly and honestly or indirectly through playing it over in your head or through fantasies? Do you express your anger in a passive-aggressive way through sarcasm? Or do you become vindictive in being silent and plotting revenge? What are the consequences of expressing your anger? This exercise can be used with other emotions to recognise how you experience these and express them.

Healthy expression of anger

To express anger more appropriately you need to check that it is legitimate and that you can express it reasonably. Ensure that you focus and direct your anger at the source, without being defensive or **passive-aggressive**. To reduce the intensity of your anger it helps to express it to yourself or a friend first. This can be done through letter writing, pounding pillows or saying out loud how angry you are. You can also rehearse it with a trusted friend through role play.

Remember to be assertive in expressing your anger and to stay calm rather than raise your voice to ensure your feelings are heard. To maximise the likelihood of being heard you could try what is known as the **sandwich technique**. This involves starting your conversation by saying something positive to the person first to show you mean them no offence, then to state your feelings, which is then followed by a positive statement. This technique is more likely to engage the person in what you have to say and ensure a more positive response.

Expressing your needs

You can adapt this process to help you to express your needs. Like feelings, your needs in childhood may have been ignored and this makes it hard for you to know what your needs are, let alone express them. You may feel ashamed or embarrassed by your needs or you may feel selfish or greedy in expressing them. Alternatively, you may fear your needs as they might reveal your vulnerability or that you will be seen as 'needy'.

It helps to remember that all humans have needs, no matter how young or old they are, and that it is natural to want to have needs met. One way of meeting your needs is to share them with other people in the hope that they will respond appropriately. Like feelings, before you can express your needs you will have to recognise them.

EXERCISE In your journal make a list of your needs. These could include: the need to feel loved, to feel respected, to have some control over your life, to have a voice that is heard, to feel safe or to be accepted. Be sure to add your own needs to this list. Reflect on these and rank them in terms of importance to you. Next consider which of these needs you can meet yourself, and which you would like to be met by others. Make a list of those people who could meet these needs and how you could express these without feeling ashamed. It helps to practice expressing your needs first before approaching the person.

When expressing your needs you must remember that while you are entitled to express your needs you cannot demand that they be met. That is the other person's choice or decision and not under your control. For this reason it is important to consider how you might feel if the other person refuses to meet your needs. While you may be disappointed, try to be objective in how you interpret any refusal to meet your needs. There may be valid reasons that your need cannot be met. Also try not to take a refusal personally and think about someone else you can ask.

TOP TIP Do not assume that one person can fulfil all your needs. It is much better to go to the right person who can most likely fulfil your needs.

Do not assume that one person can fulfil all your needs. It is much better to go to the right person who can most likely fulfil your needs. For example if you approach someone to meet emotional needs who is uncomfortable around feelings, they may genuinely not know how to meet such needs. Similarly, someone who is not at all practical, may not be able to help you with your more practical needs. It is a good idea if your support network contains people with a range of skills. This will help you choose the right person to maximise your success rather than feeling let down.

REMEMBER While you have a right to express your needs, the other person may not wish, or be able, to meet that need.

Improving communication

To help you to express your feelings and needs you need to be able to communicate effectively. It is vital that you express yourself honestly and directly. You may find the direct communication of needs difficult and tend to use **indirect communication** in which your feelings and needs are coded or hidden in mixed messages. This means that the other person has to decipher your message or crack the code. In effect they will have to read your mind. If the person is not able to decode the message then they cannot respond appropriately. This can leave you feeling not heard, rejected or resentful. Repeated failures in decoding become a self-fulfilling prophecy in which you become convinced that your feelings are never heard, that your needs do not deserve to be met.

Making sure you are listened to

To maximise being listened to, it helps to find a way of expressing your feelings or needs more directly. You will also need to check out with the other person when it is a good time to talk and decide on a mutually convenient time. This will increase the likelihood of getting your needs met rather than feeling rejected. It also helps to forewarn the person what it is you would like to talk about. This allows the person to make the right decision for them and you. For instance if the person is preoccupied with something else, or trying to multitask, then they cannot focus on you, your feelings or your needs. This will lead you both to an unsatisfying outcome.

Launching in with your feelings or needs without checking first can be problematic and will reduce the chances of your needs being met. It is better to wait and arrange another time to talk that suits you both when both of you can be fully focused. If the person says no, remember to really listen to and hear their response rather than feeling hurt and rejected or withdrawing. Be respectful of this and try to arrange another time to speak.

More **direct communication**, rather than mixed messages, or expecting others to mind read will increase the likelihood of getting your needs meet. No matter how much we might want, or expect, others to read our minds they simply cannot do this and get it right. Hoping that they will and finding that they have got it wrong will only reinforce feeling let down and feeling ashamed.

Being more direct in expressing your feelings and needs will also help you to feel more comfortable in requesting direct communication from others. This is particularly useful in requesting that others express their feelings and needs more directly, as this will reduce your need to anticipate these, or read their minds. Direct communication also reduces the need to over-analyse and over-explain, freeing up mental energy to focus on clear communication and listening to each other's responses. Ultimately, the direct expression of your feelings and needs will restore respect for yourself, without feeling ashamed or guilty.

TOP TIP Reducing the use of mixed messages and mind reading will maximise you being heard and getting your needs met.

It is also important to remember that family and friends are not expert in managing or discussing traumatic experiences. Even if they do want to help they may genuinely not know how to do this in the best way. They may fear doing the wrong thing which can prevent them from responding appropriately. Rather than rejecting you they may believe they are protecting you in case they cause further harm or damage. They may also fear becoming overloaded by your pain and hurt especially if you go into too much depth or detail. If this is the case, you may need to consider seeking professional support through counselling.

19 Maintaining self-care

As you to start to recover and begin to rebuild your life, it is important that you continue to practise everything that you have learnt. To do this you need to review your progress so far.

EXERCISE To review your progress, in your journal make a list of all the things you do now to look after yourself. Which ones give you the most pleasure or satisfaction? Which are you most proud of accomplishing? Which have been the most helpful to you? Which have been most inspirational? Are there any that you have not been able to maintain? In reflecting on these, are there any skills or activities you would like to develop more? Or are there some other self-care activities you would like to add? Could you develop these and add them to your current self-care plan?

If there are any self-care strategies that you have not been able to maintain, you might like to try some alternative ones. Or you can adapt those you have tried to suit you more. Allow yourself to be creative. The aim is to have a balance of regular exercise, rest, work and play that suits you and your needs. The focus also has to be on improving the quality of your everyday life.

The importance of play

Remember to regularly engage in activities that you can enjoy for pleasure's sake. It is really important to find time to just play. Play is a very good way of staying in the present and to enjoy the moment. This stops you from over focusing on the past or constantly worrying about the future. Now that there is greater safety in your life, you can allow yourself to become absorbed in the present and enjoy time to play. To be in the present can help you to feel more grounded and bring more peace and tranquillity into your life.

REMEMBER You cannot change the past and you cannot know the future, but you can be in and know the present.

Staying on track

As you become more conscious of how it feels to be more contented you can start to enjoy life more. Remember to be realistic though. There may be periods of time when life is more difficult or stressful and it becomes harder to maintain your self-care programme. Rather than become discouraged during these times, try to be mindful of what you can and cannot do and do not put too much pressure on yourself. Even if you attempt and accomplish only one of the things on your self-care list, that is enough to stay on track. If you feel too overwhelmed to do any, then accept that for the moment this is not possible. Once things become easier then you can start again. If you find that you start to revert to old, harmful patterns of coping you need to consider seeking professional help for extra support.

ACTIVITY To contain everyday worries you can make a 'worry box'. Write your worries down on strips of paper and put them into your worry box. This allows you to clear your mind to continue whatever else you need to do without becoming overwhelmed. This also helps to contain the weight of your worries. When you feel more able to cope, take out one of the strips of paper and spend some time problem solving that worry.

It helps to limit the amount of time you spend on worrying to about ten minutes. If you come to a solution then discard the strip of paper, if not then return it to the worry box. If you feel the worries are piling up, you could commit to spending 20 minutes a day looking at some of the worries. Then begin to problem solve at least one of them.

TOP TIP Make a 'worry box' in which to place your worries until you feel strong enough to deal with them.

Rewarding yourself

It is important to continue writing in your journal so that you can monitor your progress in achieving your goals. Remember also to record all your achievements and to reward yourself for your accomplishments. A good way to reward yourself is to make a '**reward box**' in which you place small treats to celebrate your achievements.

 ACTIVITY Make a reward box containing things that give you pleasure. These could include small chocolate treats, a scented candle, a new bath product, a new music CD, DVD, book or favourite magazine. It might also include handwritten vouchers made out to you to trade in such as treating yourself to an experience such as a massage, having a meal out with friends or going to the cinema or a special day out.

TOP TIP Make a reward box in which you place small treats to celebrate your accomplishments.

Staying connected to others

To support your self-care it is important to maintain your relationships and friendships. Regular contact with friends is crucial as it helps you to share your experiences, to have fun and to feel connected to others. Ideally try to have regular face to face contact, but if this is not possible try to stay in touch by email, text or telephone. It also helps to vary your contact with friends so that the focus is not always on talking about your recovery. Make sure that it includes other activities that are enjoyable and fun. To maintain your recovery it helps to give yourself permission to enjoy life's pleasures.

In remaining connected to others you will find that you will be more connected to yourself which will help you to maintain your self-care in making positive choices. This will include being able to say *'I want'* and *'I can'* rather that *'I am not allowed'* or *'I can't'*. Freeing yourself up from such restrictions will help you to embrace your new life and continue to flourish. Maintaining your self-care will also help you to manage any setbacks that you encounter in your recovery.

20 Preventing relapse

Maintaining your self-care can help you to manage potential setbacks and prevent relapse in your recovery. It is important to acknowledge that setbacks are inevitable and that these represent moments of vulnerability. It is important to view these as opportunities to use all the skills you have learnt throughout your recovery, rather than feeling discouraged. As some setbacks are predictable it is helpful to think about how you might manage these in advance.

REMEMBER Setbacks are inevitable and mark a time of vulnerability. They are an opportunity to use your newly learnt coping skills.

Planning for setbacks

Focusing potential setbacks in advance can prepare you to manage them more easily. Once the setback has taken hold you may become too distressed or overwhelmed to manage it as effectively. When setbacks occur it is best to go back to the basic skills you have learnt. Remember make sure you are safe and if you are not, try to put in place whatever is necessary to restore safety. Next use the grounding skills that work best for you so that you can calm yourself before tackling the setback. Talk to a trusted friend, or seek out professional help for extra support.

To help you to plan in advance for any setbacks and to make a realistic and effective action plan you will find the following exercise helpful.

EXERCISE To make an advance action plan for setbacks, in your journal record any potential setbacks or risky situations. Look at these in turn and try to predict your likely negative thoughts in that situation. Try to challenge these by checking the evidence for and against such thoughts. Next consider the behaviour which usually occurs alongside such negative thoughts or in situations of stress. Weigh up how beneficial these behaviours are and think of some alternative ways of managing the situation. Ask yourself what would make you feel better and develop you action plan from this. Remember to be realistic in your action plan so that this does not create more pressure.

Managing setbacks

It also helps to look at potential setbacks in terms of how difficult they are to manage. You could rate them in terms of: those you can manage with little difficulty, those you would struggle to manage, those that represent a minor lapse and those that you consider to be a major relapse. This will help you to rate the severity of the setback and what action plans need to be put into place.

You may find that you need to make more than one action plan depending on the situation. Once you have devised your action plan(s) record these onto a bright coloured sticky note. Stick this in a prominent place in your journal so that you can find it quickly in an emergency. When the setback occurs follow the instructions of your action plan to help you through it.

Setbacks as signals

When you have managed the setback and feel more in control, it is really important to reflect on why the setback happened and what you can learn from this. Often setbacks signal areas of vulnerability and outstanding work that needs to be done to continue in your recovery. Take note of these and try to work on that particular area so that you can feel more in control and be better prepared in the future. Also explore what you would like to do in the future and add these to your goals for recovery.

Reviewing goals

Another way to prevent relapse is to continue to measure your recovery and check that your goals are realistic and achievable. Remember to break down your goals into small measurable stages and to reward yourself as you reach each of these stages. It may be necessary to revise your goals as you progress through your recovery. You may find that you are happy to have achieved as much as you have without reaching your ultimate goal. Or you may even find that your goal changes slightly as you begin to achieve each stage.

The most important thing is to remain realistic and be open to experimenting in reaching your goals. If you are finding it hard to reach your goal, rather than see this as a setback you may need to evaluate that goal to check how realistic it is. Alternatively you might need to revise the stages for reaching that goal in the light of your achievements so far.

TOP TIP Be realistic in your goals and you can achieve them. Setbacks may be due to unrealistic goals rather than failure on your part.

What to do if you relapse

If you do relapse be sure to reduce any other pressures on you. The aim of your recovery is to reduce pressure not to increase it. It may be necessary to reduce your commitments in other areas of your life until the setback is resolved. You may need to remind yourself to say 'no' and to take more time for yourself.

You may also need to ask for help from others without feeling a failure. Seek out people in your support network who can support you through this. It is important to access as much support as you can during crises until things return back to a more manageable level. The focus has to be on reducing areas of stress and maximise stabilisation.

Assessing your level of distress

To help you assess the impact of the setback you can measure your level of distress by using the **Subjective Units of Distress Scale (SUDS)**. This scale helps you to assess your levels of distress. It is a useful aid in monitoring your recovery and can be used on a weekly basis to monitor your level of distress and to alert you to any reduction in your stability. This can help to forewarn you of changes in your well-being so that you can take action before your distress level reaches a critical point. This can help in predicting setbacks and prevent major relapses. It will also help you to compare your level of distress prior to the setback.

Subjective Units of Distress Scale

Rate yourself on the following ten point scale:

- How alert are you? (one being asleep and ten wide awake)

- How calm are you? (one being most calm and ten highly anxious)

- How well are you able to focus on tasks such as conversation, reading a book or watching TV? (one being very focused and ten not able to focus at all)

- How regulated is your mood? (one being totally normal and ten being extreme mood swings – try to include the frequency and severity of the mood swings)

- How long does it take you to get back to normal? (one being very quickly and ten a long time)

You could add to this scale by adding any other signs of your distress such as number of hours spent sleeping, increase in work hours or temptation to resort to self-harming behaviours.

Bouncing back

While there will always be setbacks what is critical in measuring your emotional wellbeing is how you handle these. It is unrealistic to expect to be free of any distress or trauma reactions and you need to accept this. The most important factor in measuring your recovery is not the amount of setbacks, but how fast you bounce back. The more skills you have to manage stress and trauma reactions the faster you will be able to restore stability and feel in control.

Remember setbacks are an opportunity to measure progress in how quickly you can rebalance your emotional state and restore stability. While you may fear that setbacks mean that you are regressing, this is rarely the case as long as you listen to the signals and take appropriate action. In addition, do not assume that setbacks will mean a return to the same intense levels of distress. This is your fear and not reality.

The skills you have learnt during your recovery will come into play and help you to manage your reactions to bounce back more quickly. Remember to trust yourself and the skills you have to cope with any setback or threatened relapse. Also try to be patient with yourself. Recovery from CSA takes time and you need to pace recovery.

WARNING If you do relapse and feel that you are in danger of harming yourself or being harmed by others, seek professional support.

21 Rebuilding relationships

As part of your recovery you may want to rebuild your relationships. This could include your relationship with your family, friends or children. Fear of intimacy and closeness can take its toll on relationships. Keeping secrets can also make relationships difficult as the fear of exposure prevents intimacy. If you were abused by a family member you may no longer be in contact with your family, or have strained relationships with some members.

A good starting point to rebuilding relationships is to monitor how you feel about significant people in your life and assess how comfortable you feel around them. From this you can assess and reassess your relationships. Those relationships that impact on you negatively may need to be re-negotiated with new ground rules, or they may need to be pruned.

EXERCISE To identify how comfortable you feel around friends and family, make a list of all the people in your life and rate how comfortable you are around them on a scale of one to five, with one being not very comfortable and five very comfortable. You can also ask yourself how safe you feel with them and how much you trust them? To what extent do they listen to you? To what degree do they respect your needs and feelings? Reflect on this list and decide who you would like to have a better relationship with and how you can rebuild this.

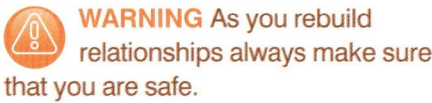 **WARNING** As you rebuild relationships always make sure that you are safe.

To help you to rebuild relationships it is important to be clear about your feelings and needs and to be able to state them in an assertive way. Look back in your journal at the exercise in which you identified your feelings and needs (see **Identifying your needs** on page 109) and add any other ones that are relevant to the relationship in question. Next think about the ground rules (see **Relationship ground rules** on page 111) that you wish to establish in rebuilding the relationship and make sure that they can be put in place.

You may also consider if there are things that you need to apologise for. In this case make sure you only apologise for those things that are your responsibility and under your control. For instance you might wish to apologise for withdrawing from the relationship, but need to explain why you needed to do this.

Reconnecting

To start the process of rebuilding the relationship you need to contact the person to discuss how you might go about this. This initial contact can be by telephone or letter to discuss a mutually convenient time to meet. If you feel you are not ready to meet face to face then consider writing a letter, or inviting a trusted friend along to support you. To maximise being listened to remember to make sure you are ready to talk and when it is a good time for the other person. Decide in advance the main points you want to make including a brief explanation as to why the relationship broke down.

Think about how you would like to rebuild the relationship and what ground rules are needed for this. Once you are clear about what you want to say, rehearse or role play it with a trusted friend to gain confidence in expressing yourself.

Some relationships cannot be rebuilt

While some people may respond positively to your wish to rebuild the relationship, others may not. Be sure to listen to the other person and their reasons why, and try to respect and accept them. Do not be discouraged if their response is negative. They may not be ready or able to rebuild the relationship right now. You can always tell them that if anything changes in the future you will be happy to discuss it with them then.

The important thing is that you attempted to rebuild the relationship. If the relationship is not repairable then you will need to grieve its loss. Be sure that you do this without self-blame. You did what you could and it was not possible for the other person.

Rebuilding family relationships

Your abuse may have impacted negatively on your relationship with your family. This is most likely if the abuser(s) was someone in the family, but can also happen if he or she was outside the family. The shame associated with CSA and the fear of disclosure means you have to detach from family members for fear of exposure. Keeping a secret is easier if you are not close to other people as there is less chance of being found out. Thus you may have avoided closeness to make sure you could keep the secret.

You may also have protected the family from knowing about the abuse to prevent bringing shame onto the family, or for fear of not being believed. This is most common in cases of clerical abuse or if you were abused by a respected member of the community. If your CSA is still a secret your relationship with your family may still be affected.

In the case of abuse by a family member your relationship with other family members will also have been affected. You may have not disclosed your abuse because you are still afraid of the power the abuser(s) has over you or other family members. Or you may wish to protect the rest of the family from punishment.

Division in the family

You may not be close to other family members, especially the non-abusing parent, because the abuser(s) has driven a wedge between you. In order to increase their power and control, abusers deliberately create a divide between family members. The guiding principle is to '**divide and rule**' as isolating you from everyone else reduces the risk of disclosure.

Your abuser(s) will have created this wedge by saying negative things about you to other family members, such as implying that you are a liar and can't be trusted. Alternatively he or she may have shown favouritism towards you to make the non-abusing parent or your siblings jealous of you. If you were isolated this way you may believe that this is your fault. This prevents you from realising that this was manipulated by the abuser(s) to increase his or her power and control.

Your relationship with the non-abusing parent

You may have felt disliked or rejected by the non-abusing parent. This may not necessarily be because they didn't love or care for you but could be due to the abuser(s) poisoning the relationship between you. You may feel angry with the non-abusing parent for letting you down or not stopping the abuse. While this understandable it is important not to blame them for the abuse. The decision to abuse lies solely with the abuser(s). If you feel let down by the non-abusing parent, it might be worth exploring whether he or she was also manipulated or controlled by the abuser(s).

The non-abusing parent may have had concerns about your wellbeing. The abuser(s) may have dispelled these by telling lies about you or making out that he or she is over-reacting or crazy. Without talking to the non-abusing parent you cannot know the extent to which the abuser(s) controlled them or other family members.

Recognising how the abuser(s) manipulated others can help you in deciding whether you want to rebuild relationships that were destroyed by the abuser(s). If the divide was deliberately created by the abuser(s) you will need to grieve the loss of these relationships. While this is painful, it can help you to decide whether or not you wish to rebuild or repair these relationships. In doing so you may have to consider disclosing the abuse.

Disclosure

Disclosure can be very difficult and painful. You are the only person who can decide to disclose and you must not let yourself be persuaded either way by anyone else, including professionals. This is a decision that only you can take. If you decide to disclose your abuse to family members you must make sure it is safe to do so. You will need to consider to what extent the abuser(s) still has power over you and other family members, and the consequences of disclosure. It is crucial that if you do decide to disclose, you explore the range of possible outcomes.

You may hope that by revealing the secret that you will become closer to your family and be able to rebuild your relationships. This is certainly one possible outcome, but not the only one.

Your family may not believe you and this could increase the divide and isolation between family members. In some cases you may be totally excluded from the family which can be another huge loss. It is important to consider all possibilities before proceeding.

EXERCISE Disclosure can be anxiety provoking and disappointing. To help you decide to disclose you need to explore your hopes and fears around disclosure and check how realistic they are. You might find that some are unrealistic, or outside your control, and need to be revised. Or you might need to let go of any unrealistic expectations, or replace them with more realistic ones. It is also important to check your readiness to disclose. If you do not feel ready to disclose yet, you can continue to work towards this and decide to do this at a later date.

Given that it is impossible to predict the outcome of disclosure you are advised to proceed with caution when disclosing your abuse. The timing of the disclosure is critical and is best left until you are well into your recovery, when you are stronger and more assertive. You need to be able to manage the reactions of various family members and any disbelief or rejection. Remember to pace yourself, and if you are not ready then do not attempt to disclose. Instead make a commitment to working on this so that you can do so at a future point.

You might also consider seeking professional support to help you prepare for disclosure. When you are ready make sure you are clear about what you want to say and what you hope to gain from the disclosure. It helps to include this when talking to family members so that you can specify how you wish to rebuild the relationship. You do not have to disclose face to face, it can be done by letter or through a third person. If you do disclose face to face you may want to have a trusted friend with you for support both during and after the disclosure.

 REMEMBER Disclosure can be disappointing and you need to be prepared for this.

Dealing with reactions to disclosure

If some family members decide they do not want to rebuild the relationship, try to understand their reasons and respect their decision. This will be painful for you and you will need to grieve this loss. They may need time to digest what you have disclosed and come to terms with it. They will need to grieve the loss of their trust in the abuser(s), and the loss of the belief that they were part of a happy relationship as well as the loss of a relationship with you. All of this takes time. If you can leave the door open then make sure that the family knows you are willing to talk in the future.

You also need to make sure that you do not impose expectations onto family members. You may want them to avoid all contact with the abuser(s), or make them choose between you and him or her. If they choose to continue a relationship with the abuser(s), perhaps you can still rebuild your relationship and only meet when the abuser(s) is not present. You need to be clear what is best for you and what you feel comfortable with and act accordingly.

Confronting the abuser

As part of your recovery you may need to confront the abuser(s). Again this can only be your decision and should not be taken by anyone else. It is crucial that you only confront if it is of benefit to you and it allows you to move forward in your recovery. If you do choose to confront you must make sure that you feel safe to do so. If you do not feel safe then don't. If it is too dangerous to do this face to face, you can do it by letter or a third party.

Confrontation is anxiety provoking and can be disappointing so it is best to be well prepared. While some abusers do admit the CSA, many deny it or blame you for the abuse. You need to be strong enough to withstand whatever the response and not let any denial erode your trust and belief in your experiences. If your abuser(s) is no longer alive, you can still confront them by writing a letter in which you express how you feel about the abuse and the abuser(s), how it has affected you and how you are now.

EXERCISE To prepare yourself for confrontation it is important to ask yourself the following questions: How can I make sure that I am safe? What do I hope to achieve in confronting? What are my expectations? What do I want to say? What is the best way of saying this – letter, telephone or face to face? When is the best time for me to confront? Where is the best place for the confrontation? What is the worst thing that can happen? How will I manage this? From this you can generate a plan of action, which you can check out and rehearse with a trusted friend. Remember the more you practice the confrontation the better you will be prepared.

WARNING Confrontation can be dangerous and you must make sure you are safe. If possible have someone with you who can support you.

If you decide to confront you may wish to do this indirectly by letter or by making an audio or video recording, which you can choose to send or not. It can help to write a letter, or make a recording that you initially do not send to rehearse what you want to say and assess your feelings. Familiarising yourself with your reactions will make it easier when you do confront. Alternatively you can confront by phone, through a third party or face to face.

If you confront your abuser(s) face to face it can help to arrange to meet on your own territory or in a neutral public place to minimise the risk of harm. You may also invite someone to be there with you when you confront to support you during and after the confrontation.

Confrontation can be very liberating even if it does not have the outcome you hoped for. The fact is that you took the risk of confronting your abuser(s) and expressed how you felt. This is something to be proud of which shows how far you have come along in your recovery and healing.

Forgiveness

As you progress in your recovery you may wonder whether you need, or want, to forgive your abuser(s). There are many different opinions about forgiveness and it is important that you explore what forgiveness means to you and whether this is important in your recovery. Forgiveness is a personal choice and only you can decide to forgive or not. Some people believe that forgiveness is necessary for healing to occur as it can bring peace. Others believe that CSA is unforgivable and that it lets the abuser(s) off the hook. To help you explore how you feel about forgiveness you might find the following exercise useful.

EXERCISE To decide whether to forgive or not, set some time aside to reflect on what forgiveness means to you. Write down your thoughts and discuss these with a trusted friend. Next ask yourself what your hopes and fears are around forgiving your abuser(s). How might you benefit from forgiveness? How would not forgiving hinder your recovery? You also need to consider the full range of your feelings towards the abuser(s). Do you have any empathy for him or her? Do you see any redeeming qualities in him or her? Do you still have loving feelings? Do you still yearn for a healthy relationship? Can you forgive some things and not others? Answering these questions will help you to be clearer about whether to forgive or not.

In exploring your feelings it is important that you do not forgive prematurely, or because of social or religious pressures. You must also ensure that in forgiving you do not reinforce your sense of responsibility, or self-blame for the abuse. You could consider forgiving some aspects of your experience and not others. For example, you could forgive the non-abusing parent for not protecting you especially if they did not know, but not if you did disclose and he or she did nothing about it.

There is no evidence that forgiveness is necessary for healing to occur. You might find it more useful to forgive yourself for not having been able to stop the abuse. Such forgiveness may be the only forgiveness that is necessary. Whatever you decide, it is possible to find peace and move on from the past, and try to rebuild those relationships that you want to make a part of your future.

REMEMBER Forgiveness is a personal choice and only you can decide to forgive or not.

22 Reconnecting to life

As you progress through your recovery you will find that you move from being dominated by a tortured inner world to one of greater calmness and stability. As you regain control of your turbulent inner world you will release vital energy that allows you to reconnect to the world. In this you will be able to appreciate life more and take pleasure in things external to you. You will find that you can greet each day anew and look forward to what life can offer you.

As you become less preoccupied with managing your trauma reactions you can also direct your attention towards others. There is considerable research that shows that helping others is an excellent way of triumphing over trauma. Helping others is a powerful aid to recovery as it gives you a sense of purpose and meaning in your life. This is a two way process, as in helping someone else, you are helped too. You will gain comfort in using what you have learnt through adversity to help someone else to feel better or manage their own adversity.

Helping others

Helping others also satisfies a number of other important aspects of your recovery. Not only does helping others feel good and provide a sense of purpose, it gives structure to your life and experience. Having something else to focus on reduces the likelihood of becoming stuck in the trauma of CSA. It will also act as a reminder of how far you have come in your recovery. This will help you to move from being defined by your CSA experience into a true survivor. Helping others also reduces social isolation, provides opportunities for connecting to others and developing companionship.

Before you commit to helping others, it is crucial that you time this carefully. It is best left towards the end of your recovery process. By this time you will have some idea of how you would like to help and in what way. Remember, you do not just have to help people who have been abused. In many respects it is best to start helping in more general terms rather than survivors of CSA as this may still be too painful. To help you explore what feels right, try the exercise below.

 EXERCISE In your journal think about some of things you could do for someone else. For example you could visit an older person, take them out or go shopping for them, take out their rubbish or help them tend to their garden. You could help children at your local school with reading, or art; if you have a specific skill you could help tutor a child. You could offer to dog walk for a neighbour, or offer to help at the local hospital or a youth group. If you feel you are ready you could volunteer with charities that help survivors of childhood abuse or rape, such as One in Four, or Rape Crisis. Or you could volunteer for Mind or Samaritans to help those with mental health problems. You could also volunteer for charities that help to protect children such as the NSPCC, ChildLine, Barnardos or the National Children's Homes (see **Resources** on page 176). Or join an action group that works on behalf of people who have been abused.

List as many ways of helping that appeal to you and rank these in order of preference. You need to be mindful that whatever you choose is manageable and best for you. For instance if you are isolated you may wish to do something that brings you in contact with others. Alternatively, if you are unable or reluctant to leave the house then consider helping over the phone or via the internet. This is a good, safe place to start and build up to face to face contact.

Knowing when you are ready to help

Before you start helping someone else you will need to consider whether you have enough energy and confidence in yourself to manage the time commitment. You will need to make sure that you can manage any anxiety or distress so that you can remain focused on the other person's needs. To help you in this you may need to ensure that you have your own support should you need it.

It is important to make sure that you choose something that will not make you feel worse. If what you choose aggravates your symptoms, or reactivates flashbacks or nightmares, this may not be right for you at the moment. The point is to reduce your symptoms and make you feel better. You may need to choose something that is not directly related to CSA as this is more likely to evoke distressing symptoms. It is crucial that you pace yourself when you help others so that you do not become overloaded or overwhelmed.

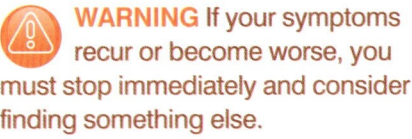 **WARNING** If your symptoms recur or become worse, you must stop immediately and consider finding something else.

Be realistic

It is also helpful to explore how much time you can realistically offer and how frequently. Will it just be a one-off offer, or would you like to help regularly? Be clear about what you can manage time-wise. It may be ten minutes, half an hour, an hour or half a day. Check whether you can manage this on a daily basis, or every two days, once a week, once a fortnight or once a month. You might start with a minimum time commitment and build up gradually over time. The essential thing is not to over-commit.

Once you have decided on how you want to help, you can start contacting individuals or relevant organisations. Before making any major commitment it is worth starting with small acts of helpfulness and check out how you feel and whether you can benefit from helping others. If you find that helping others has a positive effect on you then gradually take on your preferred way of helping. Remember to pace yourself though so that you do not rush into something which you cannot realistically commit to.

If you need to formally apply to help others, make a list of what you have learned from your abuse experiences. For instance you will have learned to be resourceful, self-reliant and independent. You will also be more sensitive to others needs and have greater compassion for others in need. Once you have identified your strengths remember to put them into positive language that emphasises your recovery, rather than focussing on the negative aspects of the abuse.

If initially people say no to your offers of help don't be discouraged or take it personally. Some people find it hard to accept offers of help as they fear it shows weakness. They might be shy about inviting other people into their life. Accept that this person does not want help at the moment and try someone else. Similarly, if an organisation is not able to take you on immediately check what will help you in any future applications.

Over time you will find that helping someone else allows you to shift your focus away from the negative effects of your abuse to helping others by making their lives a little easier. This will not only make you feel better, but also reinforce your recovery and healing.
Reconnecting to others and the world is the beginning of post traumatic growth where you are no longer immobilised by the past. It is this that allows you to embrace your future with renewed vitality in which the warrior within will triumph.

23 Justice

Dianne Ludlow
Advocacy Manager, One in Four

One in Four's advocacy service primarily supports clients through the criminal justice system (CJS) in reporting the sexual crimes committed against them as children. We also offer support in other areas, such as access to records and medical issues, but operate a flexible service on a case by case basis.

We've supported many clients through the CJS with success. Success does not necessarily mean a prosecution. It has become apparent over the years that people's reasons for finally reporting those crimes usually committed many years ago can vary. But one overriding factor which appears to be present in most cases is that of child protection. An issue which comes up for clients over and over again is the fear that other children were, or could be, hurt by the perpetrator. Some clients suffer tremendous guilt over this which is, as a victim, absolutely NOT their responsibility to bear.

Reporting the crime can assuage that feeling. The role of the police must be very clearly understood by the client so that their expectations are realistic. The police are an investigative body who will seek information and evidence which will ultimately be presented by the Crown Prosecution Service (CPS) (lawyers) in a criminal court. The burden of proof is high – '**beyond reasonable doubt**'. The case will only go forward if the two tests by which the CPS assesses a case are satisfied, i.e. a '**realistic prospect of conviction**' together with it being '**in the public interest**'. The public interest test is always satisfied in cases of sexual crimes where the evidence exists.

The police are not counsellors and their awareness of the issues involved in childhood sexual abuse will vary. Training levels around these issues is high in London, but as each police authority is autonomous there can be extreme variations around the country. The role of an advocate in such cases can, as a consequence be key to a positive or negative experience in such an emotionally loaded process. Having an advocate from an established and respected organisation such as One in Four can help. They will support and safeguard the client's rights as a victim of crime and thus the quality of service he or she receives.

As the client's advocate we are there specifically to serve them. The police generally welcome our presence and input in supporting the client to give them as much evidence as possible with which to carry out their job. As the task ahead for the client in making a statement is filled with many emotions it can be helpful if the initial contact with the police is made by the advocate. This gives a brief background of the issues involved, thus preparing all involved to foster the best working relationship to obtain best evidence.

Many historical sexual abuse cases are prosecuted successfully but inherent in the process are difficulties in gathering evidence. Some clients who report will realise that realistically the evidence they can give will not result in a conviction. The process of putting the crimes 'on the record' can be incredibly empowering. Knowing that the information has been submitted into the police intelligence database, and having some official acknowledgement of what's happened can give a lot of comfort. The most important factor in this is the knowledge and confidence that the case has been taken seriously and investigated properly. The client has finally been believed and treated with the respect they deserve.

If this has happened and the case falls on lack of evidence it may be a hard pill to swallow. However, if the client is satisfied that everything possible has been done within that process it can help in coming to terms with that.

Step by step guide to the process of reporting

The word 'victim' is used in the context of a victim of crime.

1 The crime/s must be investigated by the police in the area in which the crimes took place. It is possible to begin the process by initially reporting to any police station and that initial report would then be passed to the relevant police force/officers. As the officers at the front desk may not be trained in the subject matter it can be easier to make telephone enquiries. You will then be directed to the correct team to arrange an initial meeting. We would strongly recommend that you have a supporter with you in this process.

2 The interview stage – to make your statement you can choose wherever is most comfortable. However, most police forces now have video suite provision in an informal and comfortable setting specifically to make the victim of the crime feel more at ease. The advantage of this method is that should the case go to court this statement can be used rather than the victim having to go through it again. The victim *would* have to be cross examined in court following this, but there are also 'special measures' to minimise anxiety as much as possible (see next point).

To make your statement the police require you to give an account – to tell your story in effect. Some people imagine that it will be a question and answer session. It will become this, but you must disclose the facts and circumstances unaided by any other person first. This ensures that best evidence is given and safeguards both you and the police in possible later court proceeding.

3 Once your statement is concluded the police will begin the investigation. It may include contacting any witnesses, accessing social services or medical files and generally following any lead your evidence may give them. Under the Victims Code of Practice (easily accessed online with a search engine) you have a right to be informed of any local support organisations. You are entitled to a referral to Victims Support if you wish. You also have a right to be updated on a monthly basis. You will be informed if any arrest is made (and possible subsequent release without charge or on bail) within one to five days. Basically you have the right to be kept informed of all developments.

4 The CPS has responsibility for bringing charges under the conditions already mentioned. They also have a duty to inform you if no charges are to follow. You should also be offered a meeting with them to explain this in more depth. In practice when a case doesn't go to court it is sometimes the police who will inform the victim. If the victim isn't satisfied with the information given they have the right to seek further information from the CPS.

5 If a perpetrator is charged there will be a period of time before that case actually gets to court. Initially he or she will be formally charged in the Magistrates Court after which the case will be sent to the Crown Court for a trial date. Awaiting trial can be a very stressful time for any victim as it can take quite some time which will vary area to area.

It is not uncommon for delays to occur when the actual date is set. The courts are dealing with numerous cases and if a trial overruns then all cases are affected. Given that the victim will be building themselves up to appear as a witness in the trial, delays can be very demoralising. It is really important that a client is well supported through this period.

6 'Special measures' are available to give evidence in court. These are at the court's discretion so the CPS needs to apply for them *before* the trial begins. They should discuss this with the victim to allow time to do so. These special measures may include a screen which allows the victim to be cross examined without being seen by the defendant or a video link. This allows the victim to give evidence from outside the courtroom. There are others which can be explained to you by the CPS. Victims' identities are also protected and disclosure by the press is an offence.

7 Each court will have a Witness Service who is there to support you. This can involve visiting the court before the trial to familiarise yourself with the layout and what will happen on the day. Also they offer general information on the proceedings and personal support before, during and after the proceedings. Courts are working towards having separate entrances for witnesses and defendants. This is ongoing and not all courts are able to do this yet, mostly due to the layout of the often quite old building. The Witness Service is there to assist you in finding the best way of managing this and ideally will be able to offer a room away from the main waiting area.

Compensation

If you attend court you have the right to claim travelling expenses and the CPS should assist you in claiming this. You also have the right to claim Criminal Injuries if the crime has been reported. This does not depend on a prosecution.

Evidence will still have to be presented but the burden of proof in a Criminal Injuries deliberation is '**on the balance of probabilities**' – the civil law test. A psychiatric exam may be necessary and the whole process will take at least a year. The forms are fairly simple to complete to begin this process.

There is also the possibility of taking an action in civil law, which is a very specialised area of law. The burden of proof in civil law is '**on the balance of probabilities**' which is lower than in a criminal court. To explore the possibilities of this route you are advised to contact a specialist solicitor to discuss. The Association of Child Abuse Lawyers (ACAL) will be able to direct you to a solicitor most convenient to you. Some firms will ask you to complete a questionnaire prior to any discussion. This is in order to assess whether the rules which exist within that area of law are satisfied.

For contact details of any organisations mentioned in this section, see **Resources** on page 176.

24 Post traumatic growth

Congratulations, you have taken control of your recovery in working through this handbook. Take a moment to reflect on your accomplishments. You may wish to look through your journal entries to see how much you have achieved. Now that you have more control of your emotions, you may be less plagued by flashbacks, intrusive memories of nightmares. You may feel more in touch with your feelings, and feel more able to enjoy life's pleasures. Or you may have a stronger bond with others. Whatever your recovery has brought to your life, remember to celebrate the changes and continue to embrace your future.

At this point in your recovery you can begin to experience what is known as **post traumatic growth**. As you recover you will find that you begin to open up to further potential growth. This growth is not necessarily directly linked to the trauma. It is predominantly a result of what you have learnt through your struggle to cope with the aftermath of CSA.

Areas of post traumatic growth

Post traumatic growth can usually be seen in six significant areas of your life. The first is in your **sense of personal strength**. This is because when vulnerability coexists with an increased capacity to survive, you become stronger. Thus, while you may experience your vulnerability as dangerous or an obstacle it is also an opportunity for growth. Second is a **greater appreciation of life**, especially the more ordinary, everyday things in life. This appreciation is seen in refocusing your priorities, and spending more time doing things that are personally meaningful such as spending time with friends and family.

Now that you are more in the present, you will find that time slows down so that you notice the small details of life. You can take more time to appreciate the wind rustling in the trees or the sunlight dappling through leaves. Noticing such details can make you feel as though you are part of something bigger than yourself. Being more present also allows you to be more in touch with your bodily sensations and to appreciate the pleasure of the warmth of the sun on your skin.

Third, post traumatic growth means **getting closer to other people** especially friends and family. As you do this you will begin to value relationships more than material things or work. You will also find yourself more comfortable with intimacy, maybe for the first time ever. In reconnecting to yourself and others you feel less like an island but part of the wider world.

Your recovery will be accompanied by the fourth area of post traumatic growth, that of **greater self-understanding**. Your journey of healing is a journey of self-discovery which allows you to reconnect with your real self and strengthen your self-identity. It will also give you meaning where once there was only confusion.

The fifth area of post traumatic growth is in your **spiritual development**. When people experience life-threatening events such as trauma, they are faced with fundamental questions about the meaning of life and death. While trauma challenges all previous assumptions about life it also raises deep questions about the value and purpose of life.

These arise as a result of surviving life threatening experiences rather than some abstract or intellectual exercise. In some cases CSA, especially if it occurred within a religious context will result in spiritual injury and a loss of faith or belief. Alternatively, it can deepen your faith. Ultimately, recovery from CSA can be transforming in which resolving painful trauma can lead to experiencing life at a much deeper level of awareness.

Lastly, post traumatic growth can result in an **opening up of new possibilities** which can be life changing. A new and changed perspective on life can be the beginning of changing the direction of your life. This could be a career change, moving to a new environment or country, starting a new relationship, going back to college or a change in your priorities.

In essence, post traumatic growth can lead to a greater sense of control and purpose in your life which will help you to appreciate life even more. In embracing life you can finally move from merely surviving to thriving and flourishing and let the warrior within shine through.

Appendices

Appendix A **Notes for partners**

This section is for long term partners of survivors of CSA and sexual violence. Its aim is to look at how you can best support someone who is recovering from CSA. While the main focus is on long term partners, male or female supporting either male or female survivors, it will also be helpful for family or friends. You, as a long term partner or close friend, can play an important role in your loved one's recovery process. The best way to do this is to have some understanding of CSA and sexual violence and how this impacts on the survivor

How you can help

Learning about the effects of CSA through reading books such as this handbook or other resources (see **Resources** on page 176) will help you to understand that many of your partner's reactions are linked to the CSA. It will also enable you to appreciate how much of their energy is tied into surviving and just getting through each day. In familiarising yourself with the effects of CSA you will also show your partners that he or she is important enough to devote both time and commitment to learn more. Reading about CSA can be hard and unpleasant, so you will have to make sure that you have support in processing your feelings and thoughts. It is important that you have trusted people you can talk to, whether friends, family or a counsellor. For added support, you could also consider joining a support group for partners of survivors of CSA.

Prioritise your partner's recovery by putting his or her healing first. It is important that your partner's feelings and needs are prioritised to show him or her how serious you are in your support of their recovery process. Putting his or her needs first will also help to break old patterns of behaviour. Initially your partner will find this difficult as it is unfamiliar to them, or because they will feel they are being selfish. You will need to remind them that they have no need to feel guilty and that putting their needs first is an essential part of the healing process. This will mean that you and your needs will have to take second place for a period of time. While this can be stressful, it is critical to your partner's well-being and recovery, and ultimately for your relationship.

Supporting you partner and focusing on his or her needs can be difficult at times and you will need to ensure your own emotional support rather than putting pressure or demands on your partner. If necessary you will need to consider seeking professional support for yourself. Most importantly, remember that while change is stressful for all concerned, it can bring huge benefits and rewards.

How you can support your partner

To support your partner in the most helpful way you must be willing to find out what he or she needs. All survivors differ on what they find most helpful – some want to talk with their partner, some do not, some want to be held and cuddled while others do not. Do not assume that you know what is best for her or him. You must check this with your partner. Some survivors do not know what they want so it helps to reassure them that that is okay, and that you will check with them as you go along.

You can also show your support by helping your partner to access a range of resources, such as trusted friends, a survivor support group or counselling. This not only reduces the pressure on you but also helps to increase your partner's support network. Remember to check with your partner how much support they need from you. Some survivors want their partner to be very involved at every step of the journey, including accompanying them to their counselling sessions, while others find such level of support intrusive. It is really important to discuss what your partner needs and what you can realistically manage. If your partner does not want you to be involved, try not to feel rejected and respect his or her decision.

Your support may be most crucial if your partner decides to disclose to family or friends, or if he or she decides to confront the abuser(s). Remember you must never pressurise your partner to do this, it has to be his or her decision. Neither must you disclose or confront on his or her behalf. This is only something they can do. If your partner does decide to disclose you must make sure that your feelings about the abuser(s) do not intrude or contaminate your partner's process. If you have overwhelming feelings about the abuse or abuser(s) you will need to get support from your family, friends or counsellor. If you do seek support, remember to respect your partner's privacy by ensuring confidentiality.

Respect for your partner is essential to the healing process as it makes up for the lack of respect during the CSA. Asking your partner what he or she wants or needs is a sign of your respect for him or her. Knowing that he or she is respected can help your partner to feel more comfortable in expressing the full range of his or her feelings, thoughts and needs. You will also need to reassure your partner that you will always respect his or her privacy and not discuss their experiences or difficulties with others without permission.

Listening is one of the most powerful ways of supporting your partner, especially as no-one listened to him or her as a child. It is risky for survivors to share their thoughts and feelings as this often makes them feel more vulnerable so it is important that you honour their willingness to trust you. When listening, make sure you focus your undivided attention on your partner and be sensitive to what is being said. Let your partner go at their own pace and do not rush him or her by asking for too much detail, or by bombarding them with lots of questions. Too many questions can feel invasive, or like being interrogated, which will make your partner fear that you do not believe him or her. It is important that you do not minimise your partner's experiences, even if he or she does, and that you remain non-judgemental. Remind your partner that it takes courage to talk about what happened to him or her, and that you feel privileged that they can trust you with their experiences.

If you find listening hard you will need to be honest with your partner and try and find a way to manage this. It may help to boundary the amount of time spent discussing the CSA by setting a time limit. Listening to your partner may bring up your own childhood experiences or negative feelings. Do not share these with your partner at this point as it will shift the focus from your partner on to you. If you find that you are left with overwhelming feelings and thoughts you will need to ensure that you get support in processing these with your friends, family or counsellor.

Reassurance will help your partner to change low self-esteem and poor self-image. It is important to reassure your partner that he or she is not bad, dirty, a slut or 'damaged goods'. Many survivors put themselves down and believe that they are abnormal or unlovable. It is for this reason that you need to remind them that they are lovable, and loved. Such reassurance may need to be regularly reinforced, not just in what is said but also in actions. You will need to behave respectfully to him or her, to show how much they are valued.

It is essential that you do not blame your partner for the abuse and that you emphasise the strength and courage they have shown in their survival and recovery. Your partner may also need reassurance that you will not become impatient or leave them if their recovery is not fast enough. If your partner has any fears or anxieties it is important to listen to these and talk them through rather than dismiss or minimise them. Remember it is through listening and talking that you can reassure your partner that you are supporting him or her.

While it is important to talk about both you and your partner's hopes and fears, try not to make promises that you cannot keep. It helps to talk about your own hopes and fears as sharing your vulnerabilities can increase intimacy and closeness. This must be done in an open and honest way, without overloading your partner or shifting the focus away from his or her recovery. For example your partner might need reassurance that you will not reject him or her, while you might need reassurance that what you are doing is the right thing. It is important to explore both of your hopes and fears, and to keep a balance between these so that you keep an open channel of communication. While your partner's feelings must come first, your feelings must nevertheless be acknowledged. So as not to put pressure on your partner it is essential that you regularly seek your own source of support. This will ensure that your needs are met without feeling resentful.

How you can help your relationship

Honesty

To keep your relationship healthy it is important to be open and honest with your partner. This means being explicit when discussing your feelings, thoughts and needs. To stop your partner from mind reading it is important to share your feelings and concerns, in an honest and non-judgemental way. Remind your partner that he or she doesn't have to take care of you all the time, or that they always have to be strong. It is important that they can show their vulnerability. Many survivors feel guilty or a failure if they do not fulfil their partner's needs and will insist on pleasing them even if this conflicts with his or her own needs. Doing nice things for your partner without having to be asked, or prompted, can help your partner to learn the value of receiving as well as giving.

Boundaries

It is also important to establish boundaries and ground rules for the relationship (see **Relationship ground rules** on page 111) to ensure that your partner feels safe. This is most important in your sexual relationship. Make sure you do not treat your partner as a sexual object by understanding the impact CSA has on sexuality. It is essential that if your partner is reluctant to have sex that you do not personalise this and respect their decision. While this can feel rejecting, it is part of the recovery process to learn to say 'no' without fear or guilt. Try to avoid putting pressure on your partner for sex, or rushing him or her. To help you cope with any sexual frustration or tension, you will need to ensure that you can gain sexual relief through masturbation without feeling ashamed. When your partner is ready, you may consider engaging in sensate focus exercises to renew your sexual relationship (see **Sensate focus** on page 120).

Fears

The process of recovery can raise many fears around your relationship. You might fear that as your partner gets stronger, more self-confident or more independent that they may leave you. Or you might fear that the damage is so great that your partner might never recover. Such fears are normal and will need to be explored. If you cannot do this with your partner, you will need to do this with your counsellor or friends.

If you feel you cannot stay in the relationship don't blame your partner. Try to be honest and say you are unable to support him or her to the degree they need right now, although you may in the future. It may be necessary to take some time out so that your partner can concentrate and focus on his or her healing, while you get some support. This must be fully discussed to ensure that your partner does not see this as rejection or abandonment but as a way to support the recovery process. This can be very painful and may be best facilitated with the help of a trusted friend or a counsellor. By maintaining an open channel of communication with your partner, you and your partner can learn valuable relationship skills, which even if this relationship ends, will help any future relationship.

How to manage your feelings about the abuser(s)

It is likely that you will have strong feelings towards your partner's abuser(s). While such feelings are normal, you will need to check with your partner how to manage these. You will need to find out how he or she feels about you expressing your anger. Some survivor's find it helpful to hear their partner's outrage and anger as it gives them permission to express their own negative feelings. Others may dislike you or others expressing such negative feelings, prompting them to defend or protect the abuser(s).

Many survivors struggle to permit negative feelings about the abuser(s), and even if they do express such feelings, rarely feel comfortable when others express such feelings. This is especially the case if your partner has both positive as well as negative feelings towards the abuser(s). It is important to respect your partner's wishes irrespective of your feelings. Again to help you in this you may need to discharge your negative feelings with a trusted friend or counsellor.

What to do if your partner has contact with the abuser(s)

Managing negative feelings can be extremely difficult if your partner is still in contact with the abuser(s). Your partner may need your support and protection when visiting, or in contact with the abuser(s), which can leave you in conflict. You may wish to support and protect your partner but not want to spend time with his or her abuser(s). You will need to consider carefully whether you can be around the abuser(s), and how you to manage this. You could consider supporting your partner but limiting the amount of time you spend with the abuser(s). Or you may agree to visit the abuser(s) but not stay overnight, or reduce the frequency of contact. The important thing is to have an open dialogue with your partner to discuss what you both feel and need. If necessary, get support from a counsellor to help you manage this.

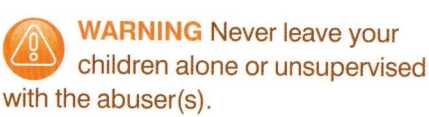
WARNING Never leave your children alone or unsupervised with the abuser(s).

If you do feel angry with the abuser(s), it is essential that your anger is focused on him or her and not your partner. Try to understand your partner's need to be in contact with him or her. It might be because your partner wants to continue a relationship with the non-abusing parent or other family members. Or it could be to ensure that your children have a relationship with their grandparents.

Talk to your partner to explore his or her primary reason(s) for staying in contact rather than assuming that it is just to have a relationship with the abuser(s). If you find it hard seeing the abuser(s), you could consider arranging to only see the non-abusing parent or other family members separately from the abuser(s). Or you could arrange to meet on neutral ground. Do not put pressure on your partner to cut all contact with the abuser(s) as this would mean that your partner will be forced to choose between the abuser(s) and you. It is far better to discuss honestly what you can tolerate and negotiate what you can both realistically manage.

To express your feelings about the abuser(s) in a safe way, it can help to write a letter to the abuser(s) which you do not send. This can also be done if the abuser(s) is dead. The letter can express your feelings about the abuser(s), how the abuse has impacted your partner, and how it still affects him or her now, as well as how it affects you and your children. Write down all your feelings about the abuse and what he or she has done, and how this has impacted on you. As you will not send the letter you do not have to censor yourself and can focus all you anger on the abuser(s), not your partner who does not deserve it.

Looking after yourself

To fully support your partner you may need to seek support for yourself. Throughout your partner's recovery you will at times feel neglected, drained, angry and resentful. This is absolutely normal, and you must not feel guilty if you feel this way. To help you manage your feelings, you need to make sure that you are supported too. You can only support your partner if you yourself feel supported. Try to be realistic in how much support you can give and be aware of the importance of pacing yourself. Most importantly, do not make unrealistic promises and make sure you acknowledge your limitations.

As recovery can be gruelling make sure you are assertive in taking timely breaks so that you can recharge your batteries. Remember if you 'burn out' then you will not be able to support your partner, and he or she will feel guilty that you have reached that point. Try to make sure you spend regular time with friends or family, and engage in activities that are not abuse related.

Do not feel guilty in seeking emotional support and reassurance as it is critical that your own needs are met through your own support network or counselling. Joining a group for partners of survivors can also be hugely beneficial.

 REMEMBER You will need support too. It will help you to have a good support network or if necessary consider seeking professional advice.

How to manage safety concerns

If you have concerns about your partner's safety, it is crucial that you seek professional advice. If your partner shows an increase in self-destructive behaviours, such as self-harm, suicidal thoughts or behaviours, or wanting to harm others, you will need to seek help for him or her. Suicidal thoughts are often accompanied with talk about burning the house down, saying that the children will be better off without them, or giving away treasured possessions and an increase in depressive symptoms.

If you are concerned that you partner intends to harm himself or herself, or someone else, you must seek professional help. You could share your concerns with your GP, your counsellor, your partner's counsellor or ring the Samaritans. If possible try to get your partner's permission to do this, if not, at least tell them what you intend to do. Remember no one can stop someone attempting suicide but seeking professional help before suicidal thoughts take hold can help that person.

 **WARNING** If you have concerns about your partner's safety you must seek professional advice.

Appendix B **Notes for professionals**

While this handbook is designed primarily for survivors to aid recovery from CSA and sexual violence, it can also be used in conjunction with the counselling process. You might find the information and exercises in the handbook helpful and could consider using them in your work with clients. You may feel your clients could benefit from reading the handbook as an adjunct to the work you are doing. The one thing the handbook is not able to provide is a therapeutic relationship in which to undo the dehumanising effects of CSA. That is where the role of the counsellor becomes critical in providing a secure base where the survivor can explore his or her ways of relating to others.

To protect you and your client it is important to develop a good practice model for safe trauma therapy. You may already have clients who have been abused, or you may be new to this type of work. If you are new to working with survivors of CSA it will be important to develop your knowledge and understanding through further specific training and reading around the topic (see **Resources** on page 176). It may also help to have a list of specialist organisations such as One in Four, or counsellors to form professional links. This is also useful if you feel your client could benefit from more specialist input.

Working with CSA

A central component of working with survivors of CSA is not judge whether or not their abuse experience is true or false. As it is impossible for you to know that, you need to stay with the survivor's feelings and beliefs about what happened. The therapeutic space is not a court of law to judge accuracy or details. What you can provide is a safe, sensitively attuned and respectful space to explore the client's experiences. In this secure base, the survivor can draw his or her own conclusion and work through any concerns or challenges.

To do this you need to have an open mind rather than focusing on confirming or disconfirming CSA. It is also crucial to remember to honour the survivor's willingness to trust you despite repeated betrayal. This indicates that hope is not extinguished and signals an opportunity to transform the dehumanisation of abuse through a human relationship. While working with survivors can be extremely tough and demanding, it is also the most rewarding work. It can be life changing for both the survivor and you.

Preparing yourself

To prepare yourself when working with survivors of CSA it is important that you gain as much knowledge as possible through specialist training and reading appropriate research. You will also need to increase your knowledge and understanding of sex and sexuality to manage the sexual elements of CSA. It is important to be able to talk about sex and sexual practices without embarrassment or arousal as this will make it easier to talk to survivors. You may also need to acquaint yourself with the role of self-medication such as alcohol, drugs or food, self-harm as well as shame. To develop self-awareness it will be helpful to explore your own value system, and attitudes and beliefs around gender issues, power and abuse.

In addition, you will need to commit to extra training and continuing professional development (CPD) as well as appropriate supervision. If necessary you can also seek consultation with someone who specialises in CSA. If there is a re-emergence of your own childhood experiences, you will need to consider returning to personal therapy. Some counsellors have found it helpful to set up their own peer support group to support each other to ensure ethical practice. All of these can be of benefit to avoid projection or contamination of the client's material.

Creating a secure base

In order to work most effectively with survivors of CSA it is crucial to establish safety first. This can only be done in a safe, secure setting in which the client can pace their recovery. It is critical that the work is not rushed, as this is reminiscent of the abuse. Try to encourage the survivor to take small manageable steps that are under his or her control. The therapeutic relationship needs to be a collaborative one in which there is mutual respect for the client's knowledge and survival so far. It also needs to be an essentially human one which is genuinely warm and caring.

To avoid disempowering the survivor, you must guard against making yourself too central to the survivor's healing by assuming you are the only one to help. You are not the only resource and it is important that you encourage the survivor to seek other sources of support such as a survivor group. This will encourage greater autonomy and help the survivor to value the coping skills and resources he or she already has.

It is also important to provide choices. Never pressurise a client to adopt what you think is best and avoid your own projections of what is right for the survivor. While your intuitions and projections are a rich source for ideas they are not the only way of healing. It is important to acknowledge that this is the survivor's process and you are merely accompanying him or her on their journey. To minimise the risk of confusion, distortion of reality and to prevent mind reading it is important to be explicit rather than leave things to interpretation. Most importantly, you must make sure that you do not make promises you cannot keep, and acknowledge your limitations.

You will also have to remain patient as recovery from CSA is not a linear process. Survivors may become distracted, or diverted or stuck. This must not be seen as resistance but as part of the healing process. Survivors find it extremely difficult to trust and they will need to test how much they can trust you. Remember that trust is not all or nothing but is something that is built over time and which will be tested along the way. Insisting on trust too early can put unnecessary pressure on the survivor and impede the therapeutic relationship.

The therapeutic relationship

The therapeutic relationship is important to aid recovery and rebuild relationship with others. The one thing you can offer as an adjunct to self-help is the warmth of a human relationship in which the survivor is valued and respected. It is that which helps the client reconnect to others. Using your own reactions to the work can be a rich source of checking how you are doing. It can also fill in what is unexpressed by the survivor.

Be careful however never to assume anything and check any perceptions, feelings or thoughts with the survivor. To keep you safe and on track, supervision will be of critical importance. If your supervisor is not experienced in working with CSA, then consider seeking additional supervision from a supervisor who is experienced in this area.

Pitfalls

Working with survivors can present a number of difficulties and it is important that you feel confident in managing these. The essential thing is that there is a good match between survivor and you. If this is not the case you must enable the survivor to make positive choices and help them to find a better match by referring them on. Try not to be despondent if it doesn't work out. By helping your client find a better match you are serving you client's needs rather satisfying your own.

Not believing

A common pitfall is doubting, or not believing, the survivor. If this occurs you must explore with your supervisor why this might be so and take appropriate action. Another difficulty is becoming aroused when listening to the survivor's experiences. While this is natural, if it becomes too frequent, or intense, then you must examine this in supervision. Remember the arousal you feel might not necessarily be sexual, but may have its origins in fear which has been eroticised. This mirrors the survivors experience in which fear during the CSA became eroticised. It is crucial that if you have such feelings that they are discussed with a trusted other.

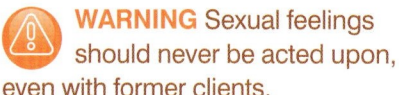 **WARNING Sexual feelings should never be acted upon, even with former clients.**

Do no harm

To avoid making the survivor feel as though they are being abused again it is important that you avoid being intrusive. You must curb your curiosity and desire to ask lots of questions, especially sexual ones as these may be solely for your own gratification. In addition, you must guard against becoming over-involved, or getting lost in the survivor's despair and hopelessness as this can lead to over-identification.

You must avoid imposing your own attitudes and beliefs onto the client.

Such things as disclosure, confrontation and forgiveness are very personal things that only the survivor can choose to do. You are there to support the survivor in their choices, not impose them. This includes imposing your beliefs on the client. This is at best unethical and at worst abusive. Moreover, it is reminiscent of the abuser(s) imposing his or her beliefs onto the survivor. To truly respect your client, you need to help him or her to restore their own reality and reach their own conclusions, independent of yours.

Given the nature of CSA it is important to be explicit around touch. Generally it is not a good idea to touch clients no matter how well intentioned, and if in doubt you must not do so. Some therapists believe that touch, if used appropriately and judiciously, can be helpful to some survivors. If you believe that touch can be of value you must make sure that you ask the client's permission, and state this explicitly at the beginning of the contract. **Sexual touch is never permitted.**

Looking after yourself

Working with survivors of CSA can be emotionally and physically draining and it is essential that you look after yourself. To avoid 'burn out', or **vicarious traumatisation**, it is critical that you seek regular supervision, as well as personal support. It is important to ensure that you have a healthy balance between work and your personal life. If possible try to balance your work with survivors and clients who have not been abused. To minimise secondary traumatic stress it is crucial to take regular physical as well as mental breaks. It also helps to take regular exercise to keep up your energy levels, and to remain embodied.

By looking after yourself you can take time to restore vitality, enthusiasm and energy. A danger when working with survivors of CSA is that this can shatter your belief in human nature, and that the world is a benign place. To make sure that this is not eroded you need to make sure that you engage in activities that help you to regain faith in human nature, and restore your zest for life.

All in all, like the survivor, you must make sure you remain connected to yourself, others and the world. With this you can truly be there to accompany the survivor on his or her journey to recovery and allow the warrior within to shine through.

Resources

Sources of help

A GP, health visitor, social worker or other professional can assist you in getting help from a clinical psychologist or other therapist. Do not be afraid to ask to see a woman if you feel uncomfortable talking to a man (or vice versa).

The national addresses or phone numbers for various organisations are listed below. For information on local sources of help contact the national office or try your local telephone directory. Please include a stamped self-addressed envelope for written replies.

Telephone helplines

The organisations listed below offer someone to talk to, advice and sometimes face to face counselling.

Childline
Children can phone 0800 1111 (free) or write to Freepost NATN1111, London E1 6BR if they are in trouble or are being abused. Also for parents, children, abusers and professionals 0808 800 5000 (24-hour helpline)

Family Matters
Counselling service for children and adult survivors of sexual abuse and rape.
13 Wrotham Road, Gravesend, Kent DA11 0PA
Telephone 01474 536 661
Monday to Friday 9am to 5pm
Helpline 01474 537 392

Rape and Sexual Abuse Support Centre
For women and men, staffed by trained female volunteers
Helpline 01483 546400 (women)
Helpline 01483 568000 (men)
Sunday to Friday 7.30pm to 9.30pm

NAPAC (National Association of People Abused in Childhood)
NAPAC is a registered charity based in the UK, providing support and information for people abused in childhood.
42 Curtain Road, London EC2A 3NH
Support line 0800 085 3330
www.napac.org.uk

Survivors UK
For male survivors of rape and sexual abuse
Helpline 0845 122 1201
Monday and Tuesday 7pm to 9.30pm
Thursday 12pm to 2:30pm
www.survivorsuk.org/

SAFE: Supporting Survivors of Satanic Abuse

Helpline for survivors of ritual and satanic abuse. Offers counselling, listening, advice and referrals.
Telephone 01722 410889

Wednesday 6.30pm to 8.30pm
Thursday 7.00pm to 9.00pm
PO Box 1557, Salisbury SP1 2TP

Samaritans
24-hour listening and befriending service for the lonely, suicidal or depressed.
Telephone 08457 90 90 90

Victim Supportline
Telephone 0845 30 30 900
Monday to Friday 9am to 9pm
Weekends 9am to 7pm
Bank holidays 9am to 5pm

Preventing abuse

Phone one of the helplines listed above or contact the following agencies if you suspect a child is being abused or is at risk of abuse, or you know of an abuser who has any contact with children.

Police

Many districts now have a special police unit that works with sexual abuse. Phone your local police station and ask to speak to the officer who deals with sexual abuse.

Social Services

Phone your local office and ask for the Child Protection Officer or the Duty Officer.

If you are abusing children or have urges to abuse children phone the NSPCC or contact Social Services or the police.

Therapy/counselling and support

One in Four
One in Four offers a voice to and support for people who have experienced sexual abuse and sexual violence.
219 Bromley Road, Bellingham,
Catford SE6 2PG
Telephone 020 8697 2112
Email admin@oneinfour.org.uk
www.oneinfour.org.uk

Action for Children
Provides national network of child sexual abuse treatment centres- providing support and counselling for children and their families. Adult survivors also.
Chesham House, Church Lane,
Berkhamstead, Herts HP4 2AX
Telephone 0300 123 2112
www.actionforchildren.org.uk

British Association for Counselling and Psychotherapy
BACP House, 15 St John's Business Park, Lutterworth LE17 4HB
Telephone 0870 443 5252 or
01455 883300
Monday to Friday 8.45am to 5pm
Email bacp@bacp.co.uk
www.bacp.co.uk

Children 1st
83 Whitehouse Loan, Edinburgh EH9 1AT
Headquarters 0131 446 2300
ParentLine Scotland 0808 800 2222
www.children1st.org.uk

Citizens Advice Bureau (part of the overall grouping Citizens Advice)
Can direct you to local groups who can help. Find the number of your nearest office in the phone book.
www.citizensadvice.org.uk

Clinical psychologists

Your GP can refer you to a clinical psychologist or you can ask another professional for advice on how to get to see a psychologist, or visit the website of the British Psychological Society.
www.bps.org.uk

DABS Directory & Book Services

DABS collate information and produce a national directory for resources for survivors. They also provide an excellent mail order service for books.
4 New Hill, Conisbrough, Doncaster
DN12 3HA
Telephone and fax 01709 860023
Monday and Friday 10am to 6pm
www.dabsbooks.co.uk

EMDR (Eye Movement Desensitisation and Reprocessing)
For information about EMDR and help to find an accredited therapist in the UK.
www.emdrassociation.org.uk

MIND
Offers individual counselling and group work.
Information helpline 0845 7660163
Monday to Friday 9am to 5pm
Email info@mind.org.uk
www.mind.org.uk

Relate
Can help with relationship difficulties and sexual problems. Provides couple counselling, face-to-face or by phone.
Premier House, Carolina Court,
Lakeside, Doncaster, South Yorkshire
DN4 5RA
Telephone 0300 100 1234
Email enquiries@relate.org.uk
www.relate.co.uk

SEREN
SEREN is a specialised counselling service in Wales for adults who have been sexually abused as children.
2nd Floor, NatWest Chambers,
Sycamore Street, Newcastle Emlyn
SA38 9AJ
Telephone 01239 711772
www.seren-wales.org.uk

Victim Support
Co-ordinates nationwide victim support schemes. Trained volunteers offer practical and motional help to victims of crime including rape and sexual assault.
Hallam House, 56-60 Hallam Street, London N1W 6JL
Telephone 020 7268 0200
www.victimsupport.org.uk.

Women's Therapy Centre
Offers group and individual therapy by women for women.
10 Manor Gardens, London N7 6JS
Psycotherapy enquiries 020 7263 6200
Monday to Thursday 2pm to 4 pm
Email appointments@womenstherapycentre.co.uk
General enquiries 020 7263 7860
Email info@womenstherapycentre.co.uk
www.womenstherapycentre.co.uk

Special agencies

ACAL (Association of Child Abuse Lawyers)
Suite 13, Claremont House, 22-24 Claremont Road, Surbiton KT6 4QU
Telephone 020 8390 4701
Tuesdays and Thursdays 10am to 1pm and 2pm to 4pm
Email info@childabuselawyers.com

ACT (Ann Craft Trust)
Provides an information and networking service to adult and child survivors with learning disabilities and workers involved in this area.
Monday to Thursday 8.30am to 5pm
Friday 8.30am to 2pm
Centre for Social Work, University Park, Nottingham, NG7 2RD.
Telephone 0225 951 5400
Email ann-craft-trust@nottingham.ac.uk
www.anncrafttrust.org

Accuracy About Abuse
Information service providing a background to media controversies.
www.accuracyaboutabuse.org

Beacon Foundation
Services for survivors of satanic/ritualistic abuse and their carers, and support for professionals.
3 Grosvenor Avenue, Rhyl, Clwyd LL18 4HA
Helpline 01745 343600 (helpline)
Weekdays 10.00am-4.00 pm

CICA (Criminal Injuries Compensation Authority)
Telephone 0800 358 3601
www.cica.gov.uk

Irwin Mitchell Solicitors
www.irwinmitchell.com

Kidscape
Information about protecting children.
Telephone 020 7730 3300
www.kidscape.org.uk

London Lesbian and Gay Switchboard
Telephone 020 7837 7324
Daily 10am to 11pm
www.llgs.org.uk

National Deaf Children's Society
Agency catering for deaf children and their families. Can offer books and information to professionals.
15 Dufferin Street, London EC1Y 8UR
Telephone 020 7490 8656
Helpline 0808 800 8880 (also minicom)
Monday to Friday 9.30am to 5pm
Email ndcs@ndcs.org.uk
www.ndcs.org.uk

Rights of Women
Informs, educates and empowers women on their legal rights.
52-54 Featherstone Street,
London EC1Y 8RT
Administration 020 7251 6575
Email info@row.org.uk
Advice line 020 7251 6577
Tuesday to Thursday 2pm to 4pm and 7pm to 9pm, Friday 12pm to 2pm
Sexual violence legal advice line
020 7251 8887
Monday 11am to 1pm and Tuesday 10am to 12pm.

Solace Women's Aid
Charity providing a range of services for women and children affected by domestic and sexual violence.
www.solacewomensaid.org

The Survivors Trust
A national umbrella agency for 130 specialist voluntary sector agencies providing a range of counselling, therapeutic and support.
www.thesurvivorstrust.org

Abuse by clergy

National Association of Christian Survivors of Sexual Abuse
An international organisation run by survivors for survivors.
c/o 38 Syndenham Villas Road,
Cheltenham, Gloucestershire GL52 6DZ
www.napac.org.uk/

MACSAS (Ministry and Clergy Sexual Abuse Survivors)
www.macsacs.org.uk

Innocent Voices UK
www.innocentvoicesuk.com

SNAP (Survivors Network for those Abused by Priests)
www.snapnetwork.org

Further reading and films featuring CSA

Self-help books for survivors

Ainscough, Carolyn and Toon, Ka, *Breaking Free: Help for Survivors of Child Sexual Abuse*. Sheldon Press, 1993, new edition 2000.

Davis, Laura, *The Courage to Heal: A Guide for Women Survivors of Child Sexual Abuse*. Bass, Ellen and Cedar, 1990.

Gil, Elian, *Outgrowing the Pain: A Book for and About Adults Abused as Children*. Rockville, MD: Launch, 1983.

Parkes, Penny, *Rescuing the Inner Child: Therapy for Adults Sexually Abused as Children*. Souvenir Press (E&A) Ltd, 1989.

Sanford, Linda T, *Strong at the Broken Places: Overcoming the Trauma of Childhood Abuse*. Virago, 1990.

Mines, Stephanie, *Sexual Abuse/Sacred Wound – Transforming Deep Trauma*. Station Hill Openings, 1996. The role of expressive and creative work in healing from sexual abuse.

Wood, Wendy and Hatton, Lesley, *Triumph over Darkness: Understanding and Healing the Trauma of Childhood Sexual Abuse*. Beyond Words Publishing Inc, 1988.

For survivors abused by women

Elliot, Michele, (ed), *Female Sexual Abuse of Children: The Ultimate Taboo*. Longman, 1993.

For black women survivors

Wilson, Melba, *Crossing the Boundary: Black Women Survive Incest*. Virago, 1993.

For male survivors

Etherington, Kim, *Adult Male Survivors of Sexual Abuse*. Pitman Publishing, 1995.

Grubman-Black, S.D. *Broken Boys/Mending Men: Recovery from Childhood Sexual Abuse*. Blue Ridge Summit, PA: Tab Books, 1990.

Hunter, Mic, *Abused Boys: The Neglected Victims of Sexual Abuse*. MA: Lexington, 1990.

Lew, Mike, *Victims no longer: Men recovering from Incest and other Sexual Child Abuse*. New York Neuramount Publishers, 1988.

For survivors with learning disabilities

Hollins, Sheila, and Sinason, Valerie, *Bob Tells All.* St. George's Hospital Mental Health Library, 1992.

Hollins, Sheila, and Sinason, Valerie, *Jenny Speaks Out.* St George's Hospital Mental Health Library. 1992.

Writings for survivors

Farthing, Linda, Malone, Caroline, Marce, Lorraine, (eds), *The Memory Bird: Survivors of Sexual Abuse.* Virago, 1996. More than 200 male and female contributors.

Autobiography

Angelou, Maya, *I Know Why the Caged Bird Sings.* Virago, 1983.

Chase, Trudi, *When Rabbit Howls.* Sidgwick and Jackson 1998. The story of a woman who developed multiple personalities to survive her abuse.

Fraser, Sylvia, *My Father's House – A Memoir of Incest and of Healing.* Virago, 1989.

Smart, P. D. *Who's Afraid of the Teddy Bear's Picnic?: A Story of Sexual Abuse and Recovery Through Psychotherapy.* London, Chipmunka Publishing, 2006.

Spring, Jacqueline, *Cry Hard and Swim.* Virago, 1987.

Fiction

Walker, Alice, *The Colour Purple.* London: Women's Press, 1983

For partners and families of survivors

Davis, Laura, *Allies in Healing: When the Person you Love was Sexually Abused as a Child.* New York: Harper Perennial, 1991.

Graber, Ken, *Ghosts in the Bedroom: A Guide for Partners of Incest Survivors.* Health Communication, 1988.

Messages from Parents whose Children have been Sexually Abused. The Child and Family Resource Group, Leeds Community and Mental Health Trust, Belmont House, 3-5 Belmont Grove, Leeds LS2 9NP.

From Discovery to Recovery: A Parent's Survival Guide to Child Sexual Abuse. Warwickshire Social Services Department, PO Box 48, Shire Hall, Warwick CV34 4RD. Audio tape and booklet.

Help with relationships

Litvinoff, Sarah, *The Relate Guide to Better Relationships.* Ebury Press, 1991.

Secunda, Victoria, *When you and your Mother Can't be Friends.* Cedar, 1992.

For therapists

Hall, Liz, and Lloyd, Siobhan, *Surviving Child Sexual Abuse: A Handbook for Helping Women Challenge their Past.* Lewes: Falmer Press, 1989.

Sanderson, Christiane, *Introduction to Counselling Survivors of Interpersonal Trauma.* London, Jessica Kingsley Publishers, 2010

Sanderson, Christiane, Counselling *Adult Survivors of Child Sexual Abuse, 3rd Edition.* London, Jessica Kingsley Publishers, 2006

Sanderson, Christiane, *The Seduction of Children: Empowering Parents and Teachers to Protect Children from Child Sexual Abuse.* London, Jessica Kingsley Publishers, 2004

Films featuring CSA

Capturing the Friedmans (2003)
The world of a seemingly typical, upper-middle class Jewish family is ripped apart by allegations of child abuse.

Hard Candy (2005)
A young girl meets a photographer via the web. Suspecting he is a paedophile, she visits his home in an attempt to expose him.

London to Brighton (2006)
A crime-thriller genre playing on the idea of social realism with the themes of child prostitution and young runaways.

Beyond the Fire (2009)
A film about love and the effect of sexual abuse by a Catholic priest.

Precious (2009)
An adaption of the 1996 novel *Push* by Sapphire.

War Zone (1999)
A teenager uncovers a secret sexual relationship between his sister and their father.

The Woodsman (2004)
A convicted child abuser must adjust to life after prison.

Useful organisations

Alcohol Concern
Directory of local advice centres and services across the nation.
Telephone 020 7928 7377
www.alcoholconcern.org.uk

Citizens Advice
Helps people resolve their legal, money and other problems by providing free, independent and confidential advice.
www.citizensadvice.org.uk

Drugscope
DrugScope is the UK's leading independent centre of information and expertise on drugs.
Telephone 020 7928 1211
Monday to Friday 10am to 4.30pm
www.drugscope.co.uk

First Signs
A self injury guidance and support network that helps raise awareness about self-injury and helps people who rely on self-injury.
www.firstsigns.org.uk

Gingerbread
Information, help and local groups for lone parents.
Telephone 0800 018 4318
Monday to Friday 9am to 5pm
www.gingerbread.org.uk

Kidscape
Kidscape produces leaflets and booklets on bullying, and runs a helpline.
Telephone 08451 205204
Monday to Thursday 10am to 4pm
www.kidscape.org.uk

Mankind
A helpline service for male victims of domestic abuse or domestic violence.
Telephone 01823 334 244
www.mankind.org.uk

National Domestic Violence
Gives information on housing, welfare, health and legal rights, refers women and children to refuges across the country, makes referrals to temporary emergency accommodation and helps to get support from the police. Free 24 hour national domestic violence helpline.
Telephone 0808 200 0247
www.ncdv.org.uk

One in Four
Offers a voice to and support for people who have experienced sexual abuse and sexual violence.
Telephone 020 8697 2112
Email admin@oneinfour.org.uk
www.oneinfour.org.uk

Parentline Plus
A free, confidential 24-hour helpline for parents concerned with a range of issues.
Telephone 0808 800 2222
www.parentlineplus.org.uk

Parents Advice Centre (Northern Ireland) – The Parenting Organisation
The Parents Advice Centre (PAC) is an organisation that provides help and support to parents facing any family difficulty.
Telephone 0808 8010 722
www.parentsadvicecentre.org

Refuge
National charity that provides emergency accommodation and support for women and children experiencing domestic violence.
Telephone 020 7395 7700
Helpline 0808 2000 247
www.refuge.org.uk

Respect
For information on national services for perpetrators of domestic violence.
PO Box 34434, London W6 OYS
www.respect.uk.net

Samaritans
National telephone 08457 90 90 90 or 020 8394 8300
Samaritans, The Upper Mill, Kingston Road, Epsom KT17 2AF
www.samaritans.org

Women's Aid Federation of England
The key national charity working to end domestic violence against women and children.
Telephone 0117 944 44 11
Helpline 0808 2000 247
www.womensaid.org.uk